Anonymus

Self-instructor and illustrated chart of phrenological and physiological development

Anonymus

Self-instructor and illustrated chart of phrenological and physiological development

ISBN/EAN: 9783741179112

Manufactured in Europe, USA, Canada, Australia, Japa

Cover: Foto ©Andreas Hilbeck / pixelio.de

Manufactured and distributed by brebook publishing software (www.brebook.com)

Anonymus

Self-instructor and illustrated chart of phrenological and physiological development

SELF-INSTRUCTOR AND ILLUSTRATED CHART

OF

𝔓𝔥𝔯𝔢𝔫𝔬𝔩𝔬𝔤𝔦𝔠𝔞𝔩 & 𝔓𝔥𝔶𝔰𝔦𝔬𝔩𝔬𝔤𝔦𝔠𝔞𝔩 𝔇𝔢𝔳𝔢𝔩𝔬𝔭𝔪𝔢𝔫𝔱.

IN the following pages, systematically arranged so as to describe the general and special characteristics of any individual, the author has adopted a new system, which, he thinks, will give much greater accuracy in delineating character and organization than by the methods commonly adopted. The usual method is simply to define as existing one out of seven different degrees of development for each department or organ, without allowing for modification of that degree, or for the peculiar way in which the faculty may manifest itself. For example, we take benevolence as an illustration. This faculty is large in the heads of many persons who are not noted for liberality, as many are sympathetic from large benevolence, but who from large caution and economy are not generous. Many are generous who from deficient social faculties and a rather coarse, rugged temperament are not sympathetic. Many have both characteristics. Again, many persons are selfish who are deficient in acquisitiveness, who do not value money, but yet give nothing to others, but use it simply to gratify their pride or passions. Many persons are ruled in their actions by large approbativeness—they are liberal because ashamed to be thought otherwise, are keenly sensitive to the opinions and criticisms of others; while many others pride themselves on being supremely indifferent to all personal popularity. Many persons are deficient of conscientiousness who perhaps lead, to all appearance, honest lives; while numbers with large conscientiousness, through strong acquisitiveness, great temptation or distress, and weak judgment, act dishonestly. The fact of these peculiarities existing in thousands of persons proves that it is at least difficult to give an INVARIABLY accurate description of each person with *seven* degrees only, and no modifications; and the following arrangement is intended, as far as possible, to obviate this difficulty by noting in the table the special phase of each faculty belonging to the person who obtains the chart.

A phrenological subdivision of the faculties was suggested and recorded on busts many years ago, Le Roy Sunderland, of Boston, U.S., being among the first to divide and subdivide some of the leading organs; and since then Messrs. Fowler and Wells, of New York, and others, have devoted some attention to this minutiæ of phrenological character, though

A

it must be conceded that for practical definitions of character it is comparatively worthless, being only valuable when used in the manner here
given, as an experienced practical examiner will judge, not by the greater
apparent development of one-half or one-third of a certain faculty, but
by the overpowering influences of other faculties, or of health and temperament, as affecting the brain. Those who profess to judge character
by minute subdivisions will certainly fail, as the forty-one faculties which
now cover the whole area of the skull, along with their groupings, conditions of health, temperament, &c., comprehend everything available
for usefulness. In defining character it is essential to avoid complication.
Clearness is the first requisite; and to be comprehensive, while omitting
all unnecessary details, is the second; and the science as it stands, along
with physiology and temperamental conditions, gives ample scope for
fully describing every individual; so that while the subdivisions are
not ignored as being in all probability scientifically true, yet in making
these divisions we must accept the modifying influences of faculty against
faculty, group against group, and body against brain, or the opposite.

In this chart I have also given five temperaments or bodily conditions,
as being more complete and scientific than the more modern definition of
three only; viz., NERVOUS OR MENTAL, FIBROUS OR MUSCU-
LAR, OSSEOUS OR BONY, SANGUINE OR ARTERIAL AND
RESPIRATORY, AND LYMPHATIC OR ASSIMILATIVE AND
SLUGGISH. These five *great* divisions of the human system seem to
fully comprehend all that is necessary in defining the general organization, along with what is termed organic *tone*, which implies fineness and
density of structure. This organic tone is a very important consideration,
and seems to embody a happy combination of temperaments along with a
spiritualized condition of brain. It is a condition that wears well, works
easily when the system is in health, gives a love of refined pursuits, is
intuitive and clear of perception, and when allied, as it often is, to
physical delicacy, gives an excess of sensitiveness to all surrounding
influences.

The individual who is described in this chart must recollect that BRAIN
POWER is directly dependent upon physical power. When the vital powers
are weak the brain is not nourished, and mental vigour cannot exist with
low physical conditions. Many a large brain shows feebleness from this
cause, but which with a return of health may show superior power.
This is true at any age, but more especially with children and old persons, or those prematurely old from physical exhaustion; and in reading
the character as described in this chart, this consideration of physical
force and present vital power is imperatively necessary.

OCCUPATION.

IN describing the occupation most suitable to the individual for whom the chart is marked, it is only necessary to mention those for which they are specially adapted. This will prevent the hesitation caused by indicating a number of pursuits; but it must be especially remembered that indicating a pursuit does not necessarily imply that the individual will EXCEL in the pursuit marked, but that it is THE pursuit best fitted to their capacities.

Many individuals are not qualified to excel in any pursuit, may have average or moderate talents only for it; but as it is requisite that their talents should be employed, the pursuit marked will indicate that which they had BETTER DO. Three crosses x x x thus will indicate they are specially fitted for any pursuit, marked two crosses thus x x that they will be successful, and one cross thus x that they have moderate abilities only for the pursuit named.

Are adapted for—

☞ In this table a dot or dash under any of the different headings shows the relative size of the faculty opposite. When a dash is made under two headings it shows that it is neither fully one or the other, but between the two; and the figures at the margin show the pages in the book where the description of the faculties is to be found. When a faculty is excessive or deficient in action, a dash is put under the head of cultivate or restrain, and the advice given in the book should be carefully attended to.

Page	CONDITIONS	Very Large	Large	Full	Average	Moder.	Small	Cultivate	Restrain
6	Organic Quality..........			a					.
7	Health, present condition		—						
8	Nervous or Mental Temperament...............				—				.
9	Fibrous or Muscular Temperament..............			a					
10	Osseous or Bony Temperament.................			a					'
11	Sanguine or Arterial Temperament..........			a					
12	Lymphatic Temperament				f.				
13	Digestive Power				•				
15	Activity				e				
16	Circulation				a				
17	Excitability				—				
17	Size of Brain...........				c				
19	Amativeness					B			
21	Philoprogenitiveness			—		o			
22	Friendship			.	a				
23	Inhibitiveness				ꞁ				
25	Continuity						c		n
27	Vitativeness			a					
28	Combativeness			a				ꞁ	
29	Destructiveness					ꞁ			
31	Alimentiveness				o				
32	Acquisitiveness		n						
34	Secretiveness		ꞁ						
36	Cautiousness		ꞁ						
37	Approbativeness		—						
39	Self-esteem.............		a					.	
40	Firmness................	ꞁ							c

The following subdivisions of the faculties are not intended to indicate that one part of a phrenological faculty is larger than another part, but simply the direction in which it is manifested in the character as controlled and regulated by the temperaments, conditions of health, or by the influence of other faculties; neither is it intended, when any of the subdivisions are marked, to show that the individual exhibits special power in that direction. The primary power of the faculty is only shown under the proper heading of large, full, average, &c.; the marked subdivision only showing the direction, which may be but feeble, the faculty itself being deficient in size or activity. The examiner must in all cases reserve to himself the alternative of marking any subdivision, as in a well-balanced brain it is not always necessary, each part being equal in power; or there may be cases of doubt as to the direction, in which case marking the size only must suffice.

As the careful marking of the subdivisions involves much extra labour and study, and can only be performed by one of great skill and experience, the charge for full marking of the subdivisions "will in all cases" be extra beyond that of the ordinary chart of character, as a faithful portrayal of these subdivisions will render a delineation much more interesting and valuable. The ordinary charge for marking these subdivisions will be 2s. 6d. in addition to the ordinary chart.

Page		Subdivisions		
19	Reproductive Love.	Love of the Sex.	Platonic Love.	Passional Love.
21	Pets and Animals.	Love of Children.	Parental Love.	
22	Sociability	Love of Family.	Gregarios Attchmnt.	Platonic Friendshp
23	Patriotism	Love of Home.	Aversion to Change.	
25	Connectedness of Thought.	Application.	Abstraction.	Prolixity.
27	Fear of Death.	Love of Life.	Resisting Disease.	Vital Endurance.
28	Defiance.	Defence.	Courage.	Argumentativeness.
29	Extermination.	Executiveness.	General Persistncy	Memory of Injuries.
31	Desire for Solids.	Desire for Liquids.	General Appetite.	Epicurean Tastes.
32	Trading and Dealing.	Acquiring General Property.	Hoarding.	General Economy.
34	Reserve.	Policy.	Evasion.	Cunning.
36	Prudence.	Solicitude.	Timidity.	Hesitation.
37	Desire for Distinction	Love of Display.	Sense of Character.	Affectation.
39	Independence.	Self-Love.	Dignity.	Hauteur.
40	Power of Will.	Stability.	Perseverance.	Stubbornness.

Page	CONDITIONS.	Very Large.	Large.	Full.	Average	Moder.	Small.	Culti-vate.	Re-strain.				
42	Conscientiousness									Circumspection.	Integrity.	Justice.	Self-accusation.
43	Hope									Speculation.	Hope for the presnt.	Hope for the future.	Exaggeration.
44	Marvellousness									Wonder.	Credulity.	Investigation.	Superstition.
46	Veneration									Respect for Superiors.	Worship and Adoration	Idolatry.	Reverence for Deity.
47	Benevolence									Sympathy	Liberality	Philanthropy.	Relief of Necessity.
49	Constructiveness									Manual Dexterity.	Contrivance.	Invention.	Verbal Constrctn.
51	Ideality									Imagination.	Refinement.	Love of Perfection	Fastidiousness.
52	Sublimity									Love of Grandeur.	Sense of the Sublime.	Expansiveness.	
53	Imitation									Mimicry.	Assimilation to Others.	Mechanical Copying.	Servility.
55	Mirthfulness									Sense of Wit.	Sense of Humour.	Love of the Ludicrous	Pleasantry.
57	Individuality									Desire for Seeing.	Mental observation.	Inquisitiveness.	External Judgment
58	Form									Memory of Faces.	Object Forming.	Artistic Regularity.	
59	Size									Estimation and Distance.	Estimating Proportion.	Judgment of Bulk.	
60	Weight									Power of Equipoise.	Sense of force in Machinry.	Mental Steadiness	
61	Colour									Recollection of Colour.	Perspective Gradation	Harmony of Tints.	
62	Order									Neatness.	System.	Love of Detail.	
64	Calculation									Recollecting figures	Estimating and Valuing.	Mathematics.	Calculating Details.
65	Locality									Exploring	Geographical Memory.	Local Minuteness.	Love of Travel.
66	Eventuality									History.	Passing Events.	Power of Associatn.	
68	Time									Chronology.	Time in Music.	Punctuality.	
69	Tune									Love of Music.	Power of Harmony	Memory of Sounds.	
71	Language									Verbal Memory.	Verbal Expressn.	Lingual Talent.	
72	Causality									Mental Suggestns.	Cause and Effect.	Desire for Knowing.	
74	Comparison									Comparing Ideas.	Physical Contrast.	Criticism.	
75	Intuition									Reading Character.	Perception of Motives	Suspicion.	
77	Agreeableness									Ease of Manners.	Blandness	Desire for Adaptatn.	

SPECIAL NOTICE.—The character, as marked in the INDEX TABLE, is described in the following pages, and the individual for whom the chart is marked should go through the book, and mark each faculty as shown under the heading in the *Index*. This will save time in after reference, and enable the person examined to SEE AT ONCE the condition or power of any faculty.

BIRKETT FOSTER, the distinguished delineator of English landscape.—High moral, intellectual, and organic quality, superior poetical conception in art.

CRAWFORD, M.P., Governor of the Bank of England.—Great practical talent, calculation, system, &c.; no imagination or brilliancy.

ORGANIC QUALITY.

Sensitiveness, clearness, fineness of tone, delicacy of perception; the artistic, poetic, and spiritualized condition.

VERY LARGE.—Are pre-eminently fine-grained and ethereal, too exquisitely susceptible to surrounding influences, are constantly liable to feel unfitted for the common and practical duties of life, without health are morbid.

LARGE.—Are highly organized and refined, and are more especially adapted for the finer pursuits, or those requiring taste. Mental clearness, with a *large* brain and health, would achieve success in the higher walks of life.

FULL.—Have a sufficiently fine tone to excel in any suitable pursuit or profession; with vigorous health and good brain power are particularly adapted to fight the battle of life, to engage in practical pursuits; and are amply developed for a position in which clearness of mental power, combined with physical energy, is required; but *with strong* passions and false habits of living may give way to some of the lower temptations.

AVERAGE.—Organic quality is simply fair; have a tendency to occasional coarseness of feeling, but with good health may resist temptation; should keep pure physiologically, avoid *habitual* stimulants, and cultivate moral and intellectual power by study and suitable associations.

MODERATE.—Are quite lacking in fineness of texture for any of the higher pursuits, and are much better adapted to gain a livelihood by labour than by study; should devote as much time as possible to culture, and avoid all gross influences.

SMALL.—Are physically gross and coarse, apt to be grovelling, uncouth, obtuse, unfit for study, and only fit for manual labour.

VERY SMALL.—Are made of dross, carnal, low, and perhaps idiotic.

To CULTIVATE.—In the first place attend to health and physical purity, avoid gross, indigestible, and bulky food, eat as lightly as is consistent with health, bathe freely, attend all means of religious and mental culture, study the beautiful and true in nature, visit picture galleries, read and think much, aspire after something high and noble and diligently follow it, and select associations higher in this respect than yourself. It should be borne in mind that from five to ten years of diligent culture will in comparatively early life change this condition of deficient organic tone from *average* to full, or even to *large*, in many persons, though this improvement depends much on hereditary qualities, and also very much on the occupation followed. A labourer may improve in a marked manner, but his opportunities will be less than a teacher or editor ; but it must be at the same time remembered that its cultivation is only NECESSARY to fit us for our condition of life.

To RESTRAIN.—Endeavour in every legitimate way to promote the animal feeling, avoid prudishness, try and be of the earth earthy, live generously, promote rest and physical ease, remember that all gross and material things were created for a wise purpose, that utility is quite as essential as beauty, and in thousands of cases more so. If this fastidious feeling is associated with delicate health, then at once attend to health. Conditions : Promote appetite, leave the dainties alone, don't criticise the style of your cooking, shun formality, be jolly, and by every means promote a healthy flow of animal spirits, and consider that what appears distasteful to you may be perfectly right and good and highly necessary.

HEALTH (PRESENT CONDITION).

Harmony of all the functions of mind and body, perfect digestion, breathing, assimilation, regularity of the heart's action, equal circulation of nervous force and heat, physical happiness, and consequent longevity.

VERY LARGE.—Are overflowing with buoyancy of spirits and life-tone, feel no aches or pains, sleep soundly, enjoy all the sensations of physical happiness, are sound as a bell, and entirely healthy.

LARGE.—Have good health, can endure pain and exposure, easily recover strength when exhausted by work, and can work vigorously, are seldom weary, and with an ordinarily active nature are most happy when fully employed.

FULL.—Have a sufficient degree of health to succeed in any suitable employment, but you must not infringe in any way by excess; you have no *present vitality* to spare, and should be regular and careful in all your habits.

AVERAGE.—Your health is precarious and will not stand being trifled with, with care will endure very well, but you are subject to ups and downs, and quite liable to break down by an extra tax on mind or body.

MODERATE.—You are too deficient of health for any permanent success, are fitful in feeling, well one day and ill the next, and may be liable to serious fits of illness.

SMALL.—Are dead and alive in feeling, incapable of any protracted exertion, and should at once use every available means to bring yourself into a state of health.

VERY SMALL.—Have hardly life enough to keep soul and body together; your life is a burden to you, not a blessing.

To CULTIVATE.—This is most important. "Without health but little can be accomplished, and you must strictly follow the dictates of nature." What you eat and drink must be perfectly suitable to the chemical, physical, and nervous conditions of your system ; a proper *dietary* is imperatively necessary. Depend on natural nutrition, not on stimulants, as nineteen out of twenty ailments proceed from deranged digestion.

Study the nature of different hygienic influences from fresh air "and appropriate baths," avoid all exhaustion, long hours of work, and, if possible, do that which is the most agreeable to do. If you are induced to take medicines and drugs, recollect that you must not uniformly depend on them, but upon the favourable conditions created by a suitable diet and drink, proper clothing and exercise, to promote an equal circulation, along with the most cheerful mental influences. There are numerous causes of ill-health, and each and every cause must be removed before the blessing of perfect or even comparative health can be ensured. The directions given in a fully-marked health table " will in most cases " be amply sufficient, along with a little sound physiological advice, to give health in all curable cases; and as to many complete health is impossible, they will also by following the rules laid down be able to realise all the health they are capable of.

To RESTRAIN "is not necessary."

BISMARK, the German Leader.—A contour denoting extraordinary powers of penetration, unflinching will, self-command, rough and determined vigour, fearless independence, along with intense individuality and originality of character; a strong capacity for sensuous enjoyments.

GLADSTONE, the Statesman and Debater.— A physiognomy at once self-reliant and fearless, indicating great mental accuracy and memory, indefatigable working power, intense practicality; without great brilliancy of imagination, but a massive and vigorous brain adapted to lead by high moral and intellectual powers.

NERVOUS OR MENTAL TEMPERAMENT.

This comprises the whole nervous system, and is indicated by mental activity, fondness for study, love of literature, reading, composition, &c.; and the physical indications are grey eyes, sharp features, a large head relatively with the chest and body, flaxen or rather light hair, sharpness of the cerebral organs, and is altogether closely allied to, and to a great extent identical with, organic quality.

VERY LARGE.—Have a nervous system strung to the highest tension, very remarkable mental activity, and are apt with a weak vital action to crowd your life into a small compass; with a good fibrous system, will show great mental endurance along with intensity.

LARGE.—Have great clearness of mind, fondness for study; are highly suitable for mental employments, and with good vital and muscular powers can achieve important results by ordinary perseverance.

FULL.—Have sufficient mental power for most pursuits; are naturally qualified to talk, write, and think well; have good mental clearness without brilliancy; may if healthy command a good intellectual position, yet are not a genius.

AVERAGE.—Have a fair degree of mental power if it is called out by culture or by circumstances; but if you give way to physical indulgences or indolence you will accomplish very little brain work. "For success" you must give the mind daily cultivation·

MODERATE.—Are mentally slow to comprehend, would not succeed well in a mental pursuit, will find it hard work to think, and will generally leave books alone.

SMALL.—Are liable to be a dunce in all that pertains to learning; brain power is too feeble for self-government, and requires direction.

VERY SMALL.—Are without ideas or thoughts, idiotic.

To CULTIVATE.—Must eat sparingly of all gross and bulky food; take a healthy and digestible diet, so that by first obtaining physical health you may obtain mental clearness. As the eagle cannot soar aloft when chained, so the brain is fettered in its flight by all morbid physical conditions: the "feeling" or desire for study will only manifest itself with an unclouded brain. Study daily and systematically, but not too long at first. Accumulate a little library, so that every spare moment may be utilised, and instead of reading or thinking carelessly commit to memory and treasure up useful knowledge that you may have an interest in retaining it. Spare no available means to attend all means of literary improvement, and remember that to get knowledge monarchs and ploughmen have to travel in the same path.

To RESTRAIN.—Cultivate the animal more and the mental less; lock up your books, bring your muscles into play, be more of an animal, think only when you cannot avoid it, systematically refrain from study, and you will find that a few days or a few weeks of complete change will repair the overworked or shattered nerves. Individuals who are living in a mental hothouse, forced to long hours of brain work by necessity, must take frequent baths, early morning walks, food easily assimilated and nutritive, and maintain their regular sleep.

FIBROUS TEMPERAMENT.

This is shown by toughness and endurance of body and mind, by size and strength of muscles, compactness of fire, capability of sustained action in walking, running in gymnastic feats, and general vigour. The outward indications are compactness of texture and an elastic, well-knit framework. It is large in all who are renowned for strength, in the representations of Hercules and the gladiators, and in such men as Blondin and Doctor Windship.

VERY LARGE.—Are as tough as the oak, and never likely to feel wearied; are made like fiddle-strings, capable of any physical strain, and if necessary could almost work day and night.

LARGE.—Have great toughness, much of the whalebone principle in you, and with a healthy vital and nervous system you will show force, endurance, and efficiency in whatever you undertake.

FULL.—Have considerable muscular power, quite sufficient for ordinary occupations, and with care and suitable training would accomplish much in the way of physical exertion without much exhaustion.

AVERAGE.—Have fair strength only, not sufficient for the long and strong pull; will occasionally feel wearied and require rest, but have quite sufficient for a light occupation.

MODERATE.—Are not likely to love labour for its own sake : soon get wearied ; should not lift and strain ; may be spasmodic and show energy, but it is likely to be fitful.

SMALL.—Appear to have no muscular strength, to be always wearied, and work is always a burden to you, and you only move when compelled to do so.

VERY SMALL.—Totally wanting in fibre and stamina ; give up before beginning : always used up.

To CULTIVATE.—Favourable conditions of health are here also important, and the cultivation should depend on occupation, whether physical or mental, for lifting ordinary weights, for rapid motion, or for mental work. Ample muscular power can be obtained by ordinary walking, skin friction, and exercise WITHOUT gymnastics. The gymnastic hobby is only suitable for cultivating for special purposes apart from the ordinary occupations of life. As every individual possesses a certain normal standard of power which a strict observance of health-laws will always call out "or develope," and extreme physical culture has the invariable effect of robbing one part of the system to feed another part, pugilists, athletes, and over-developed individuals in this respect are generally short-lived. Harmony of all parts must be strictly observed for longevity and true strength, as the man who executes whatever he attempts with ease, whether physical or mental, has more real power than the over-strained athlete who lifts tons in weight.

To RESTRAIN.—Use muscles less and brains more ; exercise only for your occupation. If naturally muscular, reduce it in no other way than by calling the vital action to another part; excessive brain work and sedentary pursuits will deplete your muscles.

OSSEOUS TEMPERAMENT.

Size and strength of bones and tendons—a large and angular frame, prominent joints, angular features, plodding but rather powerful action, not swift, yet strong, especially if allied, as it frequently is, to strong muscles. This may be called a condition rather than a temperament, and seems to arise from a certain assimilative power in the system to form bone. Many rather small-boned persons have large muscles, and some large-boned individuals are deficient of fibre, showing that size of bone and muscle are not necessarily identical.

VERY LARGE.—Are extremely awkward and ungainly, "unless muscles and nerves are equally powerful;" very slow of motion ; your overgrown frame is a burden to you.

LARGE.—Have a strong and amply-developed frame ; with good muscles, are capable of powerful feats of strength ; without good muscles, will be slow.

FULL.—Have sufficient bone power for strength and activity combined ; with good fibre, are physically harmonious.

AVERAGE.—Have not great strength of frame apart from muscular power ; should not engage in a lifting or very laborious occupation; can accomplish but little physically unless you have good muscular power.

MODERATE.—Are deficient of frame work ; too light built for any laborious work.

SMALL, OR VERY SMALL.—Have too much of the sylph nature, too tiny, and may easily have your bones broken; should only engage in pursuits that require other powers than strength of frame.

To CULTIVATE.—As bones grow or decrease as cultivated or neglected, so the first requisite is to attend to the right kind of diet. A coarse vegetable and farinaceous dietary is most suitable—milk, oatmeal, hominy, lentils, bran or shorts in bread; and the food generally supplied or grown in mountainous or rocky districts seems to contain in a larger proportion the elements of bone, as the inhabitants of mountainous regions are more bony than those in plains—perhaps partly attributable to greater physical exertion and a more bracing atmosphere, along with plenty of sunlight. A plodding, laborious occupation increases the size of bones, as is shown in the hands of labourers, navvies, &c., the bones and tendons of the hand increasing with exercise.

To RESTRAIN.—Cultivate rapidity of action; move as swiftly as possible; never plod; take a concentrated, not bulky, diet; keep the mind busy, and follow employments, if possible, in which manual labour is not requisite. Recollect that your slowness is a physical defect.

LIVINGSTONE.—Great moral and physical courage, the indomitable will, and extraordinary endurance and activity; great perceptives and exploring talent; the lion-hearted missionary.

HORACE GREELY, the journalist.—A face indicative of great clearness of mental power, warm sympathies, impulsiveness, and enterprise; not much physical endurance.

SANGUINE TEMPERAMENT.

Indicated by a rapid and strong circulation of the sanguineous fluids, along with activity and strength of the lungs and breathing power; rapid oxygenation of the blood; large chest relatively; physical excitability and restlessness, love of action, warm passions, impulsiveness, blue eyes, florid complexion, and light-coloured or sandy hair. This is essentially a recuperative temperament, giving warmth, breathing power, and energy to the whole system; it quite includes what (in other phrenological books) has been termed respiratory or breathing power, and where the sanguine temperament has not been mentioned.

VERY LARGE.—Are too fiery, impulsive, and passional; the flame of life is too fierce, "and renders you constantly liable to commit yourself, with fibrous temperament large;" have unbounded energy and unyielding strength.

LARGE.—Have great physical energy; feel a pleasure in physical motion; cannot endure confinement and a close atmosphere; are too restless for protracted study; and are too passional, unless the other temperaments with judgment control you.

FULL.—Are well developed in physical activity; enjoy action, but can be quiet if necessary, with suitable mental powers; would be most happy in an occupation demanding physical change combined with mental activity.

AVERAGE.—Are at times rather warm and impassional, but are generally disposed to be calm, with a good nervous power; should be successful in brain work; are fairly steady-going, and not too impulsive.

MODERATE.—Are deficient of warmth and physical energy; may be warmed up by strong influences, but are quite stolid and calm, and should occasionally rouse the slumbering fire; are too liable to depressing influences and colds.

SMALL.—Are quite low in animal warmth, and unless the fibrous and nervous power are strong, your rallying power will be very feeble; physical action is indispensable; are very liable to colds.

VERY SMALL.—Are inert, torpid; constantly liable to colds, and the influence of contagious or infectious diseases.

To CULTIVATE.—As this temperament embraces two great departments of the system, the lungs and blood, its cultivation is very important, particularly in cold and damp climates. Generous living is all-important—a generous vitalizing, blood-making diet, and an abundance of oxygen. A certain amount of well-cooked animal food is important, and as much bracing mountain air as possible. Low, damp localities are unfavourable. Early morning walks, deep breathing, well-aired sleeping rooms, and a sufficiently warm clothing on the extremities. Cheerfulness along with regular habits are essential; and you should not study over the midnight lamp. Over-eating is unfavourable, as a moderate quantity of food, "well digested," is better than heavy meals, "producing lightness and an inclination for exertion."

To RESTRAIN.—Live on a spare and cooling diet, avoid all fats and greasy substances, encourage the habit of thinking as opposed to physical restlessness. Don't climb or walk for the love of it, but in all things cultivate physical ease and mental solidity.

LYMPHATIC TEMPERAMENT.

Sometimes called the phlegmatic; is indicated by a slow, torpid circulation, a flaccid, colourless skin, absence of angularities in the figure or features, thick lips, a dull, quiet eye, straight and abundant hair, a tendency to abdominal fulness, and a general languor of the whole system. This temperament has by some been called a state of disease; but this is certainly an error; for though it is liable to morbid tendencies, and is often associated with scrofula and a disordered state of the lymph and blood, yet it is undoubtedly a normal feature of the system, and, along with the mental temperament, giving physical inertia and mental activity, "belongs to woman more than to man." Thousands of women have a highly-active nervous system, with an ease-loving, languid frame; and being so strongly represented in the female nature, may be truly called the great compensating balance-wheel that modifies and restrains man's restless activity.

VERY LARGE.—Are a mass of inertia; can't endure work; completely indolent · and all exercise is taken under protest.

LARGE.—Are devotedly lazy physically; may work under a strong stimulus, but you require a constant incentive to action.

FULL.—Have a tendency to be rather languid and indolent, but may master it by a strong effort; apt to hesitate and shrink from any physical undertaking.

AVERAGE.—Are sufficiently ease-loving to enjoy frequent inaction, yet may at times show powerful energy if other temperaments are vigorous. Your love of ease will only injure you if the other departments are weak.

MODERATE.—Have sufficient of this temperament for most pursuits; but if the sanguine and nervous are powerful, you should encourage it by cultivating a feeling of repose.

SMALL.—Are deficient in the love of physical ease; should not encourage a high-pressure action, but put on the brakes; avoid physical and mental worry.

VERY SMALL.—Your lymphatic system has no control over you; with much sanguine power are liabe to be a piece of perpetual motion.

To CULTIVATE.—As the lymphatic condition is that which gives repose, it is necessary to resolutely control physical restlessness as you would curb a restless steed; everything must be done deliberately, and no new or unnecessary sphere of action must be sought. The demand for its cultivation indicates too much hurry and perpetually worrying over details. "Make up your mind to let well enough alone. Try and increase your weight by hearty eating and plenty of sleep. Take only one step where you usually take two." In short, be as calm and indolent as you possibly can be, remembering that the world was not made in a day, and that a long, quiet, and happy life is more desirable than a short and feverish one, combined with the wealth of a Crœsus.

To RESTRAIN.—Eat seldom, and take very little bulky food; give yourself plenty of work to do, and create work that must be done, and do it; systematize your time for work; keep a good timepiece, and never let it get ahead of you; encourage deep breathing, and excite sanguineous power by a somewhat stimulating and energizing dietary. Don't indulge in long sleeping. Recollect that many great men have achieved wonders with but four or five hours' nightly sleep. Take shower-baths; keep the skin active; and act in every way so that you will at length feel a pleasure in the mere performance of whatever you undertake.

DIGESTIVE POWER

Is indicated by a freedom from all heaviness after meals either in brain or stomach, a hearty enjoyment of food, and a healthy appetite that instinctively craves whatever is most suitable to the demands of the system.

VERY LARGE.—Your digestion is perfect; can eat all ordinary food with the keenest relish; and you are not likely to be reminded that you have a stomach.

LARGE.—You have excellent digestion; a freedom from all heaviness after meals; are essentially hearty.

FULL.—Your digestion is generally good, but not the best; are liable now and then to have attacks of indigestion, unless you are careful in diet.

AVERAGE.—Have rather imperfect digestion. Each violation in too much food, or wrong food, reminds you of your error by dulness or distress in the front part of the brain.

MODERATE.—Will find much difficulty in selecting suitable food. Over-eating or hasty eating always distresses you.

SMALL, OR VERY SMALL.—Nearly all kinds of food disagrees with you, and you are always being reminded that you have a stomach; feel very wretched after meals.

Precocity, or great mental activity, a highly restless intellect, and strong moral or religious tendencies; a capacity for art, music, and general scholarship; only moderate digestion.

Not precocious, a happy disposition, lymphatic, and ease-loving; good capacities; solid but slow of development; good digestion.

To CULTIVATE.—As the proper digestion of food is indispensable to health, so its cultivation is of the greatest importance. The chemical condition of the stomach must be first considered, whether alkaline or acid, and if either, "a dietary of the opposite chemical condition must be taken." If the blood is poor in quality, and unfit to form a vigorous gastric secretion, the meals must not be bulky; and with a sluggish liver plenty of time must elapse between meals. Cold dishes of all kinds, sodden pastry, pork, ham, veal, duck and goose flesh, all fibrous meats, fats, and oily substances, cheese, newly-baked bread, rich sauces, boiled pastry puddings saturated with water, undercooked cabbages, potatoes, and other vegetables, all excess of slops, and badly-cooked food of every description must be avoided. Eating slowly is indispensable. The admixture of saliva with the food while in the mouth is the first process of digestion. And all solid food should go into the stomach thoroughly insalivated. Never eat till you are hungry and can enjoy your meals. If you have no appetite for a meal, wait till the next meal; never eat under the delusion that it gives you strength whether you are hungry or not. More food than can be digested is a source of weakness, not strength. If you feel a sinking and gnawing sensation at the stomach frequently, it is an indication that you want food, and solid, well-cooked food slowly eaten is in nearly all cases the best, though in many cases where there is a sensation of thirst nutritive liquids may be freely taken. Hot drinks as well as cold dishes should be avoided; and avoid following any hobbies in reference to any special class of diet. A mixed diet is best for the stomach, the same as a *variety* of studies and recreations suit the mind; but a change is positively necessary to a weak stomach; and if any special article of food is craved for, let it be indulged in moderately. Avoid running after patent pills and quack remedies; they give temporary relief and future misery; for it must be remembered that what the vital powers of the system require is simply no obstruction, and sufficient abstinence is imperatively demanded in indigestion. If you take four meals a day and suffer, cut off one meal; if you still suffer with three ordinary meals, take two instead; and in rare cases, with a very sluggish circulation and sedentary habits, health may be restored by one meal only, as a contented mind is a continual feast, and digestion is partly a nervous action; so never eat heartily with an over-worked or anxious brain; the strictest temperance is essential during all periods of grief or deep trouble; in short, to have good digestion wait till you are hungry, if the period is only three hours or twelve; for healthy hunger indicates digestive power. Follow nature, avoid eating from mere habit, and remember that as one mind differs from another in its slowness or rapidity of thought, so one man's stomach may execute its function of digestion twice as rapidly as that of another; so that along with a proper diet healthy digestion may be considered as almost uniformly relating to the length of time elapsing between our meals.

To RESTRAIN is not necessary.

ACTIVITY.

This is a condition dependent upon form, density of structive activity of brain, and general tension of the whole system; it is indicated by restlessness, love of action for its own sake, continued motion even in sleep; it is shown on the cranium by the lateral projection of the bone at the back of the head called the occipital spine or spinous process.

VERY LARGE.—Are as restless as the wind; find it impossible to keep still; can't endure the least confinement or restraint.

LARGE.—Are continually changing your position; are unhappy if you cannot be moving, and can only be quiet by a strong effort.

FULL.—Are happy when active; with good health, are generally going; but can be calm and quiet with a moderate effort.

AVERAGE.—You do not love action for its own sake, are rather inclined for repose capable of action, yet are rather plodding and steady-going.

MODERATE.—Can sit or remain still for a long time in one position; do not like over much bodily exertion.

SMALL.—Will not take more steps than you can help; dislike activity; are likely to be physically too easy-going for your own good.

VERY SMALL.—Are a waddler; fond of lounges and easy-chairs; hate all physical exertion.

To CULTIVATE.—Employ similar means to those laid down for the cultivation of the sanguine temperament, as the most powerful forces in nature are those which are the swiftest. Remember that your inertia destroys your power; if too stout, walk it off. Lay out a systematical routine of physical action for each week or month. Cultivate action according to the demands of your pursuit or avocation.

To RESTRAIN.—Endeavour to increase your weight avoirdupois; cultivate your easy-chair; remember that your extreme restlessness is a state bordering on disease, an over tension of nervous and fibrous action, and that the human frame was not intended to be a perpetual-motion machine; live generously, and cultivate contentment.

CIRCULATION.

This is also a condition dependent on the size and activity of the brain, and the general strength of the whole vital system. In many cases the *heart* is small, and of itself not nourished. A good circulation is indicated by an invariably equal warmth all over the body, and a power of resisting cold—what is termed rallying power; its absence, by cold extremities, generally a hot brain, or local heat, and chilly sensations.

VERY LARGE.—Have a remarkably strong and uniform distribution of heat all over the body, never take colds, and have no liability to ordinary sickness.

LARGE.—Have an excellent circulation, equally warm hands and feet, and are well adapted to cold latitudes.

FULL.—Your circulation is commonly good, are quite comfortable with exercise; but will suffer occasionally from cold extremities if you are sedentary.

AVERAGE.—You will require to improve your circulation; are subject to rather cold hands and feet, and to palpitation of the heart from extra exertion, occasional headache, or a rather dry and clammy skin.

MODERATE.—Have a poor circulation; flashes of heat and chill, are easily affected by changes in the weather—chilled by cold, and overcome by hot weather; subject to palpitation and headache.

SMALL AND VERY SMALL.—Have a weak, irregular pulse, fluttering at the smallest excitement; subject constantly to brain fever; and are a perfect thermometer in feeling—always either up or down.

To CULTIVATE.— The clothing must be ample, especially on the extremities; woollen is the mos suitable, and so fitted to the body that exercise can be freely taken. Brisk walks should be frequently taken. The feet must be kept warm by sufficient covering—thick stockings and well-lined boots in damp or cold weather; a good walk just before going to bed; if not, hot foot-baths; sponge or light shower-baths at morning if a warm, healthy glow follows. Do not chill the blood by heavy cold baths; use friction upon the skin with a crash towel, and see that you have an ample ventilation of fresh air into your apartments to feed the lungs with oxygen. It must be remembered by sedentary persons, females and others who suffer by cold feet and extremities, that the cold air is always at the lower part of the room; and unprotected feet and limbs, by having merely cotton covering and flimsy boots, drives the blood back upon the chest and brain, laying the foundation for consumption, brain fever, tic, neuralgia, headaches, and a host of complaints; and delicate, chilly persons must also remember that if they live in a cold climate instead of a warm one, they must dress warmly all over their bodies, not around the chest only, so that the vital heat in their system will be maintained to the same degree as if *in* a warm latitude.

To RESTRAIN.—This is not really necessary; yet if the glow of heat is so great to the surface as to cause inconvenience, "turn as amphibious as possible by bathing in cold water."

EXCITABILITY.

This is owing to both physical and mental causes—to sharpness and angularity of the brain, to constitutional weaknesses, and to a low state of health acting upon a highly-strung organism.

VERY LARGE.—Have excessive excitability; are over-strung like a stringed instrument strained to the point of snapping; may be liable to insanity.

LARGE.—Are quite too excitable with deranged health, are incessantly annoyed by trifles, and are constantly liable to lose all self-possession; with large caution will be miserable.

FULL.—You are generally too excitable for your own good, but yet may control yourself by a strong effort and a little philosophy. Should study the laws of health.

AVERAGE.—Are only excitable at times, generally calm and self-possessed; with good health may seldom or never suffer from it.

MODERATE.—You are generally calm and stolid; do not easily lose your balance; can be cool when many others are upset, or very much excited.

SMALL.—Are as stolid as the Indian; are always calm; are like a rock, immovable.

VERY SMALL.—Are completely devoid of excitability.

To CULTIVATE is not generally necessary, though if too stolid may be regarded as having no sympathy; should merely cultivate earnestness.

To RESTRAIN.—This is important, as self-control is indispensable to success and happiness. The diet must be nutritive, but cooling; all heating food and alcoholic liquors must be rigidly avoided; engage in no business of chance or luck, on gaining or speculating; no business of trusting or giving credit promiscuously; never speak till you can command your feelings; read much on practical philosophy; use sedative baths; drink little or no tea or coffee, wines or spirits, as a beverage, and firmly resolve to live so calmly that you will live long, as all excitement hastens on the functions of life with dangerous rapidity. In short, *be cool!* Leave tobacco for the dullards, feverish enthusiasm for fanatics; politics and speculation for the ambitious; hobbies for the mountebanks; and keep yourself for practical every-day usefulness.

SIZE OF BRAIN.

Size is indispensable to greatness, but not always to brilliancy; and size of the brain must not *always* be predicted from its possessor wearing a large hat. Depth of convolutions is equally important, and *quality* more important. Partially-educated individuals in mental science have laid too much stress on external tape measurement. Organic quality and health, as well as harmonious balance between brain and body, are most important. Thousands of average-sized heads surpass those that are large from having superior health, harmony, and quality. Idiots have possessed large heads; and clever, talented men in certain spheres have had only moderate craniums. Commanding greatness requires both size and quality, as large brains always have and always will govern the world, as throughout the universe power is given by size. Much dependence has been placed by some on phrenometrical and tape measurements of the head, but for practical purposes they are useless and misleading. To judge of real brain power the experienced examiner must grasp every condition, physical and mental; must have no hobby of mere size and shape to ride upon, but must be able at a glance to sum up the maximum of power of brain. Constitutional weakness and their effect, the influence of cultivation or its absence, in short, as swiftly read every condition as he would determine the size of ONE faculty. Healthy, well-balanced heads may range from 20 to 24½ inches in circumference, each powerful in proportion to size and quality; and brain may range in weight from 40 to 62 ounces. Woman's brain about one-fifth less than man's.

VERY LARGE.—With a well-balanced temperament, good health, and superior quality, are capable of becoming an intellectual giant, of taking the lead wherever you go; will be endowed with wonderful clearness and force, and can mould others to your will. With a sluggish temperament will be great on occasions, as much depends on activity, as well as on culture and education.

LARGE.—Are capable of rising to eminence; with good brain quality and health will be able to control and govern; with large perceptive organs will stand high in practical shrewdness, and will show superior talent in carrying out whatever is congenial to your leading powers; with a weak physical frame will be fitfully great; and with an indolent temperament will only show greatness when roused by a strong incentive; are capable of much good or evil according to the relative superiority of the higher or lower faculties.

FULL.—Have a brain capable of much power; with an active temperament, good quality, and harmony of the faculties, may excel in scholarship or business; will not sway a commanding influence, but may show even brilliancy; without culture or much activity will pass through life unnoticed; but with great energy and practical talent can hardly fail in realizing solid success in the occupation most suitable.

AVERAGE.—If activity and health are good, will be capable of holding a good average position in whatever sphere you are by nature fitted; but should not attempt to compete in any pursuit if not thoroughly adapted to it. With deficient self-confidence, are liable to be controlled by others. With great energy, may even shine in one or two things; but should aim at perfection rather than versatility.

MODERATE.—Your success in life will depend on quality of organization and health. With a coarse temperament, are fitted only for the lower pursuits, and will require to have your judgment directed by a superior mind. With a brain harmoniously balanced, good quality, and culture, are fitted for the lighter and finer pursuits, and may show much taste in copying others; but are not original or profound, are likely to be unsteady in opinion, and impulsive in action.

SMALL, OR VERY SMALL.—Are too weak mentally for self-government; with low quality, are quite idiotic.

In estimating character it is highly necessary to judge of the peculiar manner in which the different faculties manifest themselves. A faculty acting by itself is a blind instinct; but this never occurs in an harmoniously balanced brain. Many animals have infallible instincts from the superior size of certain faculties over others. Man's intelligence does, or should, proceed from no excess of one part over another. When this is the case it gives rise to a perversion. A large intellect with a deficiency of spirituality, reverence, &c., leads to a supernatural or spiritual disbelief. A perfect balance of the two will investigate, but never utterly reject, what the intellect cannot comprehend. The moral brain recognizes spiritual laws. The intellect investigates those laws, and harmonizes them with our material conditions and what are termed natural laws; so that it is unsafe to place great stress upon the action of one large faculty, when other faculties exist equally powerful. Character and disposition are determined by the balance of parts; and in the marking of this chart attention must be paid to this balance, or the influence of one class of faculties as opposed to another class. And the marking of the faculties should be, not always in accordance with their exact size on the cranium, but as according to the influence of other faculties they manifest themselves in the character.   Taking the faculty of *amativeness* as an example, we give it one or more of four directions, and the same with every other faculty, and this "special direction" is determined by the overpowering or influencing power of other parts of the brain.

Louis XVI. of France, the sensuous voluptuary.—Face indicates vanity, haughtiness, insincerity, intellectual weakness, and love of sensual gratification.

M. Thiers, the brilliant and versatile orator and writer. — A contour of great harmony, health and power; a capacity for excellence in any sphere; not severe, but pliant and sympathetic.

AMATIVENESS.

Love for and attraction toward the opposite sex.

1st. Reproductive Love.—Leads mankind to a desire for the continuance of the race.

2nd. Love of the Sex.—The tendency to love and admire those of the opposite sex from a strong sexual feeling, and principally shown by the depth of the faculty upon the neck.

3rd. Platonic Love.—A love for the sex strongly regulated by high and pure feelings ; caressing and fondling.

4th Sexual Excitability.—Emotional love, caused by an impulsive and overwrought nature ; rather liable to morbid fancies, hysteria, and nervous disease.

Very Large.—Have an almost uncontrollable desire for the opposite sex, a depth and intensity of passion that requires rigid attention to health, and strong moral force to resist.

Large.—Have deep and powerful sexual attachments, are capable of the most intense pleasure in the society of those of the opposite sex who are congenially constituted; with health and a good degree of moral and intellectual force, are capable of exciting the most ardent and devoted love in others.

Full.—Are capable of much sexual fervour and love, but there is not that depth and intensity that exercises a continuous influence over the feelings; are often ardent, but occasionally are (apparently) cool and indifferent to sexual love.

Average.—With ordinary health are capable of evincing a good share of sexual love, but will be only capable of attracting the few, not the many; with strong intellectual and moral power would only have sexual love excited through admiration.

MODERATE.—Could live an unmarried life without serious inconvenience, have (in health) a sexual desire easily gratified; with spinal or morbid irritation of the glandular and nervous system, may have considerable of sexual excitability, perhaps hysteria.

SMALL.—Are almost like an iceberg in love matters, likely to be prudish, and care nothing for the opposite sex apart from admiration of talents or ordinary friendship.

VERY SMALL.—Are sexually *idiotic;* should never marry.

To CULTIVATE.—As it is certain that the proper cultivation of this faculty is as necessary and important as that of any other, it is only essential first to understand the amount of regulating force in the character; for the purity and benefit of society, it must always be suitably controlled by what are termed "higher faculties," such as conscience, judgment, benevolence, &c.; but as very many men and women are cold and indifferent in married life, it must be acknowledged that amativeness is either insufficiently developed, or that two have been joined together who should have been always separate. In children where it is defective they should not be brought up exclusively with their own sex, but allowed freely to mingle with the opposite. A child brought up constantly with old persons is liable to have this faculty dwarfed; its healthy development can only be secured by having the instinct guided by the invigorating influences of a healthy companionship, and it must be remembered that its proper development is essential to a manly or womanly character. Many from its deficiency are unsuitable for marriage, and if married grow miserable and unhealthy. Those who are deficient should recollect that prudery and sexual stoicism is a morbid and inharmonious condition, and that it is neither manly nor womanly to be devoid of attraction toward the opposite sex, as prudes of both sexes are invariably shunned or hated. Attention to health is important; living rather generously, avoiding all perplexing care and overwork, studying the human form Divine as artists do, and living as far as possible in an atmosphere where are attractive and winning members of the opposite sex. And if marrying, wed one who is somewhat more strongly developed in the sexual passion.

To RESTRAIN.—If the cultivation of this faculty is important, then its proper restraint is more so, as it is the basis of all that renders married life what it should be; so, when abused, it is the source of frightful misery, morally and physically. In every civilized country numberless unprincipled quacks continually fatten on the calamity of sexual abuses. These pretended philanthropists, *alias* social vampires, are the most dangerous enemies of those who suffer from sexual abuse; but to properly restrain this faculty, the young of both sexes should early be taught certain important principles in physiology, for a large amount of mischief is done at a comparatively early age. Parents and guardians of the young should be fearless in pointing out probable and certain errors, and with a general knowledge of those sciences which explain the human system this could easily be done. A healthy education is imperatively demanded on this point; and whenever a morbid excitability is manifested, health should be immediately attended to; the diet should be unstimulating and regulating; highly-seasoned food and exciting drinks should be avoided; clothing should not be in excess, but so warm as to preserve an equal heat throughout the body; the mind drawn to intellectual and moral culture; and while the blandishments and society of the opposite sex may not be entirely neglected, let the one great resolution of *"self-control"* be the animating principle of life.

PARENTAL LOVE

Implies love of pets—children and animals—and all young and tender objects. We give it three conditions :

1st. PETS AND ANIMALS.—This is shown by the greater development of the lower part of the faculty.

2nd. LOVE OF CHILDREN.—Shown by the more ample development of the upper part, along with a higher moral and intellectual nature.

3rd. PARENTAL LOVE.—Implying the desire to be a parent, and is shown by the greater width of the faculty, along with a certain conservative tendency in the character to surround oneself with permanent objects of affectionate interest.

VERY LARGE.—Are passionately fond of all children and pets, and are constantly liable to idolise and over-indulge them. To rule children will require an excellent judgment and a strong will ; without these would be most successful in spoiling them.

LARGE.—Feel a strong tender parental love, and can easily win the affections of children or household pets, as a parent would be tender and indulgent.

FULL.—Under ordinary circumstances would be rather indulgent and affectionate toward children and pets; but if temper is irritable will occasionally be impatient or hasty with them ; with sufficient benevolence are otherwise well adapted to be a teacher or parent.

AVERAGE.—May love your own children rather fondly, but your affection for and treatment of them is much influenced by your general disposition; with irritability and not large benevolence are apt to be rather harsh.

MODERATE.—Have not sufficient of this faculty to undertake much parental responsibility, are apt to consider children and pets in the way, and if deficient in sympathy may neglect and injure them by indifference or harshness.

SMALL.—Will feel very little interest in children and pets ; are not suitable for a teacher or guardian; with large benevolence may not be unkind, but yet quite indifferent.

VERY SMALL.—Are apt to hate children, and had better undertake no responsibilities concerning them.

To CULTIVATE.—To do this it is necessary also to stimulate benevolence, remembering that children are helpless and innocent, and cannot thrive without affection and sympathy ; study the artless and winning ways of the dear little ones, that from their pure natures would instinctively love you or shun you ; learn to regard a child-hater as a monster unfitted for the domestic hearth ; go with them, instruct them ; teach them to love you for your gentleness, so that you may learn to reciprocate their love by a devoted interest in whatever is pure and innocent in human character. If you aim to gain a livelihood by teaching, recollect that even with otherwise high capabilities the deficiency of this faculty would render you a failure.

To RESTRAIN.—In order to overcome excessive affection it is necessary to exercise a strong will and all the judgment at your command, recollecting that a spoilt child is often a calamity. Study the differences in children around you, and learn to carefully observe all the natural faults, as carefully and firmly correcting them ; let no appeal turn your judgment aside from the path of duty. Promise no more than should be given, and fulfil punctiliously all that you promise. Avoid corporeal punishment, as the after remembrance of it is apt to react painfully on yourself;

but treat children as simply responsible and intelligent beings that demand your aid and attention from a practical sense of duty, and nothing more, and whatever your sound, untrammelled judgment resolves on doing, that *do*.

SCOTT.—A face in which social and intellectual power are strongly blended; great will, hope, penetration, and large friendship.

Chief Justice COCKBURN.—Intellectual power predominating over the social; immense perception, memory, energy, courage, and directness; intense individuality of character.

FRIENDSHIP.

Attachment to society, friends, love of companionship, and ability to make friends. We give it four conditions:

1st. SOCIABILITY.—Power to win in general society; to be equally and generally friendly with all.

2nd. LOVE OF FAMILY.—Attachment to one's own kin, to relatives, brothers and sisters.

3rd. CONJUGAL ATTACHMENT.—Permanent and lingering attachment for one object, and great grief and unhappiness when separated from it.

4th. PLATONIC FRIENDSHIP.—Which regards friendship with great purity of motive; a friendship based much on honour, as *Damon* and *Pythias*.

VERY LARGE.—Are devoted to friends with indescribable tenderness; everything that mars or interrupts friendship is most painful, and with large sexual love would regard life as wasted if not ruled by constant love.

LARGE.—Have a highly sociable nature, which if unrestrained by other conditions will make your friendships sincere and lasting; without large caution and reserve will often form hasty attachments.

FULL.—Are of a social disposition, and may form hasty attachments, but can separate and form new friendships without much difficulty; can occasionally be happy and satisfied if apart from friends.

AVERAGE.—Have a rather friendly disposition, but it is largely modified by other circumstances; with strong selfish faculties will not sacrifice for friends, but with large benevolence and sympathy are quite likely to do so, yet the ruling influence of other faculties may often drown the voice of friendship.

MODERATE.—General society is very apt to be distasteful, can easily live apart from friends, and have too little power to excite true and disinterested friendship in others.

SMALL.—Are cold and often very unsocial, with large reserve; are liable to be a recluse or misanthrope.

VERY SMALL.—Are a stranger to friendship; cannot understand what it means.

To CULTIVATE.—Remember that without the amenities and attractions of social life the world would be a desert, and society would fall into disintegrated atoms, each atom heartless and selfish in its complete isolation. You should learn to value the true friend, and by sympathy and straightforwardness of motive induce others to regard you as worthy of their esteem and friendship. Never remain alone voluntarily. Cultivate your intellectual, moral, and all other faculties in association with others. Throw off all reserve, and fully trust some one. If deceived, do not rail at the heartlessness of friends, but try again, recollecting that the principal difficulty may have been in your own coldness. If unmarried, marry, "if possible," one whose sincerity and devotion will win you in spite of yourself; and remember that thousands climb the ladder of success, not so much by their talents, as their magnetic power of winning confidence through a sincere and positive friendship.

To RESTRAIN.—This is especially necessary where the character is not endowed with prudence and high moral force. False friendship is yearly the ruin of thousands; it substitutes feeling for judgment, is constantly warped and misled. If your friendship is very strong, the study of human nature is indispensably requisite. Treat all whom you do not fully know with suspicion till you discover their motives. If you are strongly persuaded, and are uncertain how to act, seek honest and intelligent counsel. Learn the art of freezing up occasionally, and absorbing yourself with books or other occupations that will wean you from social temptations, remembering that the health of thousands is destroyed, and many thousands of naturally honest individuals are rendered dishonest by yielding to the blandishments of persuasion. Learn to say, *No.*

INHABITIVENESS.

The patriotic instinct, or love of home. We give this faculty three conditions or phases:

1st. PATRIOTISM.—Implying love of country and its institutions, and evinced by a combination of reverence, firmness, self-esteem, along with a full development of the upper part of inhabitiveness.

2nd LOVE OF HOME.—Fondness for the domestic hearth, a place of one's own to live in, and shown by a retiring, perhaps quiet disposition; aversion to general company, and fulness of the lower part of the organ adjoining friendship.

3rd. AVERSION TO CHANGE.—A liking for sameness of position and place; the same bed, easy-chair, place at table, &c., shown by general order and regularity of habit, with a fulness in the outer part of the faculty.

VERY LARGE.—You have such an intense love of home that away from it is certain to render you home-sick; are miserable away from it, and can fully appreciate the immortal melody of " Home, Sweet Home;" are a natural patriot.

LARGE.—Will soon become strongly attached to the place you live in, and leave it with great reluctance; with large reverence are likely to be very patriotic.

FULL.—Have a sufficiently keen enjoyment of a good home, and will leave it with reluctance; yet are attached to it from friendship or other causes quite as much as from the inhabitive feeling.

AVERAGE.—Have some regard for your home, but not enough to induce you to cling to it when interest or duty called you away. Could easily change your home from the influence of other attractions.

MODERATE.—Can easily change from place to place, and become a rambler and cosmopolite. Care for home only on account of its associations.

SMALL.—Are not likely to form any home attachments, and with strong powers of observation are likely to grow passionately fond of travel.

VERY SMALL.—Could be as migratory as an Indian, a rolling-stone—here to-day, there to-morrow.

Kosciusko, Polish Patriot.—A face indicating enthusiasm, powerful feelings, and devotion; love of home, friends, and country; great perception and force of character, but not strong reasoning qualities.

Lord Derby, the Patrician.—A truly noble face, indicating great will, pride of character and race, large benevolence, and superior intellect; a face devoid of all littleness and meanness.

TO CULTIVATE.—The improvement of this faculty is somewhat difficult in this age of travel, when the world is being opened to exploration. But the true method of cultivation will lie in first deliberately securing a good home; secondly, in rendering it as fascinating and attractive as eye and hand can make, and surrounding it with interests and responsibilities in such a way that no special temptation to leave it will exist; and recollect that the highest realization of human happiness can only be found at the domestic hearth. Resolve that if all the rest of mankind are turned out of doors you will have a sacred shrine, over the portals of which no monarch can enter without your permission.

TO RESTRAIN.—It is necessary to scrupulously avoid the selfish feeling of thinking your own home is all the world. Think of how narrow-minded you are certain to become. If able, travel whenever possible, and learn that the world is full of interest and beauty far away from your own little homestead. Interest yourself in subjects that imperatively demand your attention elsewhere, and try and find frequent pleasure at your neighbour's hearth; recollecting that this exclusive isolation and absorption in the walls of one little tenement is neither noble nor healthy, and is equally shared with you by the ignoble and selfish cat that will not desert her corner for her best friend.

CONTINUITY.

Power of abstraction, and ability to hold the mind to one process of mental action; connectedness of thoughts and ideas. We give four conditions :

1st. CONNECTEDNESS OF THOUGHT.—The power to arrange thoughts and ideas in harmonious connection with each other.

2nd. APPLICATION.—Studious attention to one thing at a time till finished; assisting perseverance of character.

3rd. ABSTRACTION.—The power or tendency of becoming so completely absorbed as to lose all mental or physical perception of all surrounding objects and sounds.

4th. PROLIXITY.—The tendency to be tedious in explanation or argument, evinced by a general slowness of mental action, along with the natural action of the faculty.

VERY LARGE.—Are liable to be so excessively prolix and tedious as to wear out the patience of all persons of energy; can leave nothing unfinished; have wonderful patience, but no point or conciseness.

LARGE.—Are quite able to apply your mind for any length of time on one subject. With a slow temperament, are likely to be very tedious. With great activity, may be both brilliant and admirably connected in all your plans and ideas.

FULL.—Are generally disposed to attend to but one thing at once, yet with ordinary mental activity can turn rather easily from one thing to another; are neither disconnected nor yet tedious.

AVERAGE.—Have a fair degree of connectedness, but will often feel a difficulty of thinking long on one subject. With an active brain, are much more versatile than continuous. Thoughts sometimes go rambling.

MODERATE.— Are perhaps too fond of variety of thought, and of thought and occupation. Are not confused by change, and without great firmness and good mental training will be superficial, changeable, wanting in solid application.

SMALL.—Are constantly liable to fail in fully carrying out your plans and ideas. With an active front brain may be a Jack-of-all-trades, beginning everything and finishing nothing. Will require to make an extraordinary effort to keep persistently on one track.

VERY SMALL.—Have no continuous power, and if destitute of firmness and executiveness will be a complete shuttlecock in the hands of fate and circumstances.

To CULTIVATE.—With persons engaged in certain occupations this is extremely difficult, such as shopkeepers and those whose minds are constantly on the alert with new duties. Isolation and study is indispensable, and one or two hours daily should be rigidly devoted (while alone) to some connected train of thought and memory—the study of mathematics, history, metaphysics, or poring over mechanical and ingenious contrivances. Chess-playing is an admirable means of cultivation, were it not considered a waste of time. Many with a small amount of this faculty are brilliant and versatile, but never profound; and it may be suggested that for many pursuits in life its cultivation is not essential, as when too large it unfits one for the changing panorama of human action; but a certain amount of it is indispensable to a clear and consecutive memory, its deficiency causing mental fickleness; and it must be distinctly borne in mind that a systematic and daily cultivation of the other faculties, during the hours when the brain is most vigorous and capable of receiving impressions, is imperative. Historians, chronologists, astronomers, metaphysicians, and all deep and profound thinkers, must be more or less possessed of this faculty in full development, and the daily systematic study of such men's productions is valuable. To be alone, to contemplate, to force the mind into daily abstraction with some absorbing subject—to arrange all your plans, business matters, and thoughts consecutively, so that each link of your life's method of action will harmoniously connect with each kindred link, until the complete chain by which the mind is governed has every link in its proper place, and your fitful, changeful reveries cease.

To RESTRAIN.—The prolixity induced by the excessive action of this faculty renders thousands of persons tiresome bores in society; they are always going, going, but never gone; always finishing, but never wind up; and their harp has only one string which wearies by its verbose monotony. Those who are troubled with it should keep an excellent timepiece, and keep everything they do, and all that they have to communicate, within fixed, moderate limits; avoid amplification and detail; recollect that the age is impatient, and demands brevity; consider yourself entitled to a rebuff or reprimand if you unconsciously buttonhole any friend or man of business; call upon the man of business only at the proper time to do business; do your business without affix or prefix, and leave him at once to attend to his own business; never preface what you are going to say, but say it, and don't repeat it; always do to-day what MIGHT be left till to-morrow; be ahead of time, not behind it; let swiftness, promptitude, and dispatch characterize all your movements, recollecting that the world is rushing on while you are prosing and keeping others from getting ahead.

SELFISH PROPENSITIES.

A group of faculties located directly around the ears, giving width to the head and general force and impetus to the character. Their abuse leads to gluttony, drunkenness, selfishness, malice, quarrelsomeness, and deception. Their proper use is to protect and conserve our own interests, and regulated by intellect and moral qualities to evince force and energy on all that the higher faculties dictate.

NELSON, the fearless Commander.—Great will, small caution, deficient acquisitiveness and love of life.

DANIEL DREW, the liberal and energetic American. — Great acquisitiveness, energy, benevolence, with prudence and wariness; large love of life.

VITATIVENESS ·

Gives love of physical existence, tenacity of life, and dread of annihilation. We make four conditions :

1st. FEAR OF DEATH.—Implied by general timidity, great sensitiveness to pain, and accompanied by the fulness of the outer part of the faculty next the ears.

2nd. LOVE OF LIFE.—A keen sense of individual being, living and enjoying life, and is partly indicated by a general cheerfulness and physical buoyancy.

3rd. RESISTANCE TO DISEASE.—The capacity to resist contagion or infection of whatever character, to stand climatic changes, and indicated by a vigorous circulation and pure blood.

4th. VITAL ENDURANCE.—Power to endure fatigue and recuperate vital force rapidly by sleep and rest.

VERY LARGE.—Are passionately desirous to live for the sake of being: would have a horror of annihilation even though intensely miserable; with an ordinarily good constitution would have wonderful power in resisting the encroachments of disease.

LARGE.—Are very tenacious of life; are full of the *elixir vitae* that buoys up and sustains the physical frames, and unless sustained by a strong sense of religion would dread death as a terrible calamity.

FULL.—Will cling to life with much tenacity, especially if otherwise healthy ; with moral and intellectual faculties large, will value life for the sake of high achievement; without these will only appreciate life for the social and other pleasures that it affords.

AVERAGE.—Are perhaps sufficiently attached to living to occasionally dread the thoughts of death, but would value life from other causes than mere love of it ; if ill or miserable would perhaps wish to die.

MODERATE.—May love life, but are not very anxious about living ; with affections blighted and hopes crushed would almost regard death as a welcome messenger.

SMALL, OR VERY SMALL.—Have little or no regard for life ; if unhealthy will regard it as a burden ; if gloomy and miserable are likely to contemplate suicide.

To CULTIVATE.—In order to do this, it is necessary first to create within us and around us something worth living for. Life should not be aimless, purposeless; health and vigour of body should be first. attended to, as valuation of human life is often in proportion to a good digestion. It is said that a man once shot himself because, being passionately fond of muffins, his stomach refused to digest them ; but disordered nerves and digestion causes thousands to regard life as not worth the minimum pleasure and maximum trouble it brings. After once having established health, occupy your mind with something so congenial that you must insist on living till each achievement has demanded something else more noble and worthy ; by this you will learn what the Creator gave you life for. You should never sate yourself with any pleasure so far as to blunt the appetite for it; fully employ your time, and learn to regard yourself as a responsible living being, whose duty it is to encompass within your life all that a rightly-constituted human being should be proud of achieving.

To RESTRAIN.—To do this successfully life must be directed to the accomplishment of useful and noble objects, and the spiritual existence or life to come should be often dwelt upon till you learn to realize that the present existence is only a fleeting and transient passage to a higher condition. Try and emulate as much as possible the asceticism and self-denial of the martyrs and pioneers of Christianity and civilization, regarding yourself as a probationary founder of that which the wise and good would seek to copy and imitate ; in short, do not live for selfish aims and physical pleasures only, accept them only so far as they are necessities of life, but regulate and define them strictly by all the moral powers you possess; by so doing the life you value so much may be nobly resigned for a martyr's crown.

COMBATIVENESS.

The faculty which gives physical courage, resistance, and the feeling of self-defence. We give it four conditions:

1st. DEFIANCE.—A fulness in the lower part, giving a daring, aggressive, and contentious spirit.

2nd. DEFENCE.—A more ample development of the front part, giving the disposition to resist encroachments and physical difficulties.

3rd. COURAGE.—A happy combination of other leading faculties, such as firmness and moral power, that give coolness and heroism.

4th. ARGUMENTATIVENESS.—The faculty acting in conjunction with an active and critical intellect giving the love of intellectual controversy.

VERY LARGE.—Are very prone to be continually at war with others, are extremely contrary and resentful, and if caution and judgment are weak may do hasty acts of violence; with these large may show prudence along with great boldness and daring.

LARGE.—Have a resolute, courageous nature fond of attacking and being attacked, yet if benevolence is large may easily forgive, but without due regulation by the higher faculties will often show rashness and irritability of temper, will boldly meet opposition.

FULL.—Will seldom shrink from opposition; are likely if your temperament is excitable to be too fond of it; with good health may be generally quite pacific, but with disordered health are not likely to be over amiable; are quick-tempered at times, but without great provocation will not be contentious; have enough courage to meet all ordinary difficulties in life.

AVERAGE.—Are generally pacific, but when driven to it will defend yourself and your rights boldly; if moral faculties are large will show more moral than physical courage; if caution is large are often likely to be over timid.

MODERATE.—Are too apt to avoid collision and show less pluck than you need; with caution large will have too much of the negative amiability: and if firmness and self-esteem are deficient are too likely to be trampled upon; may have moral courage only.

SMALL.—Are inclined to be quite cowardly, too tame to fight the battle of life, and if hope is low and caution large will be extremely desponding and chickenhearted.

To CULTIVATE.—The improvement of this faculty depends largely on occupation. There are pursuits in life which if followed directly encourage and promote it. In literary life, those who are censors and critics; barristers, and those in the political arena; in commerce, such as commercial travellers; and in every day life, all those trades and avocations where great difficulties have to be struggled with and overcome, so that those deficient should devote a portion of their time in contending with some difficulties demanding personal courage. Individuals with this deficiency are often about as successful as the proverbial "Pus in Gloves," and their timidity often renders them the prey of bolder and more designing spirits. Young men who are deficient should avail themselves of all such means as debating institutions, gymnastics and field sports; and young women, along with direct improvement of physical health, the want of which is frequently a great cause of *little* courage, should aim at something important and suitable to their abilities, and then daily struggle for success. *Healthy* physical and mental opposition should be continually sought; if others succeed, resolve that your success shall be greater than theirs. There is no need of any needless and irritating aggression, for sufficient pluck can always be achieved by boldly struggling in the ordinary avocations of life, and where the case requires a courage beyond what this will supply seek out and devote yourself to something specially heroic.

To RESTRAIN.—First ascertain the cause of your irritability or ill-temper; it MAY lie in disordered nerves to some extent ; for it must be remembered that a healthy frame and healthy nerves have generally a full degree of self-control, and as an irritable temper poisons all domestic happiness, so the attainment of perfect health must be the first object. Many thousands lose their tempers easily when out of health; with health, they can stand the chafings of trial and misfortune more calmly and nobly. If inclined to be irritable, always debate the propriety of speaking before a word is uttered, or avoid speaking altogether, remembering that noble passage, " that he who ruleth his temper is greater than he that taketh a city." Persons who are too actively developed in this faculty should thoroughly study human nature, and by so doing they will learn that uniform kindness and benevolence has a talismanic influence to reach every heart; that all persons are different, and require different modes of being reached and influenced ; should learn, as far as is consistent with truth and honesty, to be "all things unto all men."

DR. GUTHRIE, the Scottish Orator and Divine.—A face portraying great sympathy, geniality, imagination, humour, and power of representation, combining strength and nobleness of character.

A WESTERN INDIAN.—An organization indicating selfishness, cunning, ferocity, memory of injuries, the denizen of the wilderness, and hater of civilization ; no originality or humour.

DESTRUCTIVENESS, OR EXECUTIVENESS.

The power which gives thoroughness, force, severity, and desire to exterminate and overcome. We give it four divisions :

1st. EXTERMINATION.—The back part of the organ adjoining combativeness gives severity and the destroying tendency.

2nd. EXECUTIVENESS.—The front part gives efficiency and force in either physical or intellectual achievement.

3rd. GENERAL PERSISTENCY.—The middle part gives perseverance, in conjunction with firmness.

4th. MEMORY OF INJURIES.—This phase arises from full or large destructiveness, uncontrolled by sufficient benevolence and sympathy.

VERY LARGE.—Are liable to be vindictive and revengeful, perhaps a *terrible* temper when once aroused; and, unless well endowed with prudence and benevolence, are likely to be so bitter and implacable that forgiveness may be unknown to you.

LARGE.—Have great force of temper and determination when aroused; opposition only adds to your force in overcoming obstacles; without benevolence prominent will be revengeful; with large firmness, are both forcible and obstinate; but with large moral powers and good judgment will evince your executive power in the right direction.

FULL.—Can witness pain or death, but are not likely to show an over amount of severity, except with deficient benevolence and an excitable temperament; but in ordinary matters will require considerable provocation to call out your severity.

AVERAGE.—Are not deficient of the feeling of indignation, but are usually rather forgiving; if benevolence is large, will have no difficulty in forgiving, and almost forgetting, injuries.

MODERATE.—Are generally quite mild, perhaps not often forcible enough. If combativeness is deficient, are likely to be quite tame; and with much benevolence, cannot cause or witness pain or death.

SMALL.—Are decidedly weak in the power of executing. Your anger is but momentary, and if combativeness is deficient, and caution large, will be excessively timid and fainthearted.

VERY SMALL.—Are unable to fill any position requiring force, and have the utmost feebleness in your anger.

PIERRE BONAPARTE.—Great destructiveness, selfishness, and brute force; with deficient moral powers.

REV. J. STACK, the kind-hearted and self-denying missionary.—Small selfishness, great liberality, deficient self-esteem, and high moral powers; small destructiveness.

To CULTIVATE.—In this age of competition, when so many thousands are struggling for supremacy, the cultivation of this faculty is most important, especially when regulated, as it invariably should be, by the higher dictates of humanity; and no unnecessary harshness need be shown while doing so, for the struggle for success, in which all the faculties are strained up to vigorous action, will give executive power. When deficient in children, they should be encouraged in all healthy sports. Where competition and physical vigour are demanded, their mothers should adopt the Spartan method of training; and they should never be allowed to give up the achievement of any undertaking which they are capable of, and which is proper for them to do. They should be taught rather to seek difficulties than shun them. They need not be *forced* to witness pain or death, as this faculty can be sufficiently aroused in other directions and by other means; and as the legitimate action of this faculty lies in the vigorous execution of all that we undertake, so let no undertaking be abandoned, but by good judgment and invincible resolution gain force and impetus by going on from conquering to conquer.

To Restrain.—The abuse of destructiveness lies in malice and unforgiveness, resulting frequently in murder and terrible crimes. Its restraint is not difficult if benevolence is large, and the whole nature otherwise is sympathetic; but if these are deficient, the task is rendered highly difficult. Thousands of individuals strive to forgive while asserting that they cannot forget the remembrance of an injury; even if *it is* what is termed "*forgiven*" does not constitute COMPLETE FORGIVENESS; and in that sense forgiveness is impossible, unless memory was razed cut from the brain. But the true mode of restraining destructiveness lies in the cultivation of benevolence and reason. You should learn that malice and revenge are instincts of the lower animals, and too mean to be harboured by a noble mind; and you should learn that the law of love is a thousand times stronger than the law of severity and force. Parents should never punish their children while they themselves are angry, and children too large in this faculty should never have their hate aroused by undue or degrading punishment. The sympathetic study of human nature is the most direct and powerful method of restraint, as by so doing we can always discover a key by which the most obstinate nature can be overcome without the intervention of brutal punishment, and if rightly studied it teaches us the highest of all the Christian virtues— "charity."

ALIMENTIVENESS.

Sense of hunger and thirst, and the desire to gratify the appetite. We give it four conditions:

1st. Desire for Solids.—Shown by the superior size of the back part of the organ.

2nd. Desire for Liquids.—As indicated by a greater fulness in the front part.

3rd. General Appetite.—Indicated by a rather active digestion, good health, and general sense of solidity and plainness.

4th. Epicurean Taste.—Shown by a fastidious disposition, acute nerves, sensitiveness to uncleanliness and disorder.

Very Large.—Are constantly liable to eat and drink too much; to excessive indulgence of the pleasures of the table; without a strong will to give restraint, are apt to be a glutton.

LARGE.—Have a keen and hearty appetite, a genuine relish for the pleasures of the table; occasionally liable to over-eat, unless the digestive organs are very powerful; with unfavourable health, condition may frequently suffer.

FULL.—Have a good appetite, enjoy food, but are not over-disposed to indulgence; can restrain yourself if necessary; with a suitable dietary, are only disposed to eat to live.

AVERAGE.—Have a fair enjoyment of food, but are disposed to be rather particular; with morbid conditions of hea .h, are likely to have a rather indifferent appetite.

MODERATE.—Are frequently liable to nave a poor appetite and to neglect your palate; with weak nerves, are apt to be morbid and fastidious.

SMALL.—Are apt to often regard food with dislike; have generally a wretched appetite; constantly liable to neglect meals.

To CULTIVATE.—First ascertain from your general state of health and occupation what class of food you most require, and also from the sluggishness or activity of your glandular and nervous systems how frequently you should eat. If there is a predisposition to excess of alkaline juices, with a rapid pulse and wasting tendency, you should adopt the habit of eating little and often. If the condition, on the contrary, is acid and congestive, with a slow pulse and bilious tendency, eat seldom, and partake principally of solids. If you do not know what class of food is most suitable to you, consult some hygienic physiologist on the subject. Avoid what are termed "wholesomes," and the adoption of all extreme views in regard to suitability or unsuitability; follow nature, and partake of ALL kinds of well-cooked and digestible food in moderation, varying the dishes rather frequently; should not prepare your own food, and should always have what you eat, however simple, tastefully cooked, and learn to think of partaking of your meals as a necessary adjunct to health and physical comfort.

To RESTRAIN.—As a large majority of ailments and diseases spring from over indulgence in eating and drinking, it is necessary to strongly exercise judgment and will, and learn only to partake of the exact amount necessary for the repair of the body and brain. Thousands of fine intellects are blunted and ruined by over indulgence; and those engaged in pursuits requiring much mental work and anxiety should learn that a clear brain and a healthy life can only be secured by moderation, and the dietary must be rigidly kept to that point that leaves the brain clear and unclouded. Meals may be occasionally omitted; don't regard mealtime as necessarily involving the duty of eating, and do not labour under the fallacy of supposing that quantity of food invariably gives strength. More than can be fully digested is weakness and disease, not strength. Eat only when hungry, drink only when thirsty; strictly limit quantity, and avoid the temptation of special feasts, remembering that all gluttony is a degrading weakness that depresses and clouds the mental powers, shortens life, and invariably entails after misery and discomfort.

ACQUISITIVENESS.

Love of property, desire to accumulate, and provide for the future. We give it four conditions:

1st. TRADING AND DEALING.—Giving the disposition to speculate in property, and fondness for general dealing.

2nd. Acquiring General Property.—The love of acquirement arising out of intellectual, artistic, or ambitious desires.

3rd. Hoarding.—Treasuring up, without reference to trade, either money or other valuables, such as the miser, the antiquarian, or bibliomaniac.

4th. General Economy.—The faculty under the proper control of other feelings that simply gathers from necessity and wastes not.

Very Large.—Are apt to make money or other property your idol; without great conscientiousness and sense of character will be constantly tempted to acquire dishonestly; with deficient benevolence, are disposed to be miserly and selfish.

Large.—Have a strong desire to acquire property; frugal and particular in your dealings, will regard it as a sin to waste; with large benevolence, will give judiciously, but not wastefully; with large conscientiousness and sense of character, will be honest and scrupulous, but will set a high value on money and property.

Full.—Will accumulate property both for itself and what it procures, yet are not penurious; are usually saving, yet supply your wants; with good moral and intellectual power, are not likely to be at all mean; and if benevolence and friendship are large, are often liberal; with these faculties deficient, are apt to regard charity as always beginning at home.

Average.—With a good degree of caution and prudence are sufficiently fond of money and property, but can spend freely when necessary. If the temperament is indolent, are not likely to push forward with sufficient vigour in accumulating. With great energy may accumulate property, but care less for it when obtained. With large intellectual or social power, would accumulate only to gratify other faculties.

Moderate.—Will find it much more difficult to keep money than to make it. Will not grieve much over its loss, and unless necessity imperatively demands, are likely to be careless or over-liberal.

Small.—Are often liable to spend your money very foolishly, quite profuse and careless, unless higher faculties rule you. Without caution and judgment well exercised will be prodigal and reckless.

To Cultivate.—To improve this faculty it is necessary to create needs and wants. Those who have no incentive to action, no demands beyond the personal wants of their own individual existence, will find accumulation a difficult task. You should first set up an object for accumulation, whether intellectual, moral, or social. A great lawyer once, while pleading his first case in court, felt his courage beginning to decline; but at that moment he imagined his children tugging at his coat tails, and it instantly aroused him to greater confidence and power. If you wish to accumulate money or any other property, some special object of attainment demanding money for its realisation should be at once promoted. No squandering for any other dispensable object should be allowed. If a home is demanded, let every available shilling go to swell the home fund. Learn to save the pennies for the sake of the pounds. Pay as you go, rigidly accounting for all outlay; and whatever may be the weekly or yearly earnings, let there be a surplus untouched. Remember that millionaires have started in the world on sixpence, or less; and it will be wise to recollect the fact that old age will come along apace, when a feeble body and brain can no longer work and accumulate. And fancy yourself at that period homeless, perhaps friendless, looking back retrospectively over hundreds and thousands foolishly wasted, that, if saved, would have given friends, home, comfort, and length of life.

To Restrain.—In order to do this it is necessary to study the real object and philosophy of life, that true happiness is not achieved by accumulating wealth till we are surfeited with the cares and anxiety it brings. You should recollect that few of the *very rich* are happy; that the highest pleasure is realized by a judicious and liberal use of all that the Creator has given to us. A wit once remarked, on hearing that a certain person had died worth a million, "Well that is a good sum to begin the next world with." Thousands become so absorbed in money-getting that health is ruined ; and accumulating at last becomes so necessary to their existence that when from necessity they resign business and money-getting, for want of their usual stimulant of action they begin to die. If you find yourself growing too fond of money, set yourself at once to the acquisition of some attainment that will afford you pleasure and interest when work and business are resigned. Let it be music, art, literature, or something important within the scope of your abilities, and by and by you will find it a haven in which old age can revel with satisfaction and delight. If too anxious about accumulating for old age, insure your life for as large a sum as you can afford, and then live fairly up to your income ; but whatever you do never allow your whole soul to be absorbed in the circumference of a sixpence, remembering that you cannot carry your gains with you into another world.

BARON LIEBIG, the Chemist and Scientific Discoverer.—A face denoting high reasoning and investigating powers, strong mental activity, great earnestness, enthusiasm, and vigour, along with shrewdness and business capacity ; open and frank.

HOME, the Spiritualist.—A face indicating much imitative cleverness, secretiveness, and acting talent ; a natural capacity for excelling in legerdemain and in deceiving the senses ; a lover of mystery, but not a philosopher.

SECRETIVENESS.

Power of concealing our thoughts and feelings ; policy and evasion. We give it four conditions :

1st. RESERVE.—Indicated by fulness of the front part, and giving the power and desire to appear indifferent, to keep still and listen.

2nd. POLICY.—Fulness in the middle part, giving the disposition to watch and evince tact in turning everything that may occur to a good account.

3rd. EVASION.—Fulness of the back part, and, along with other conditions of the faculties, gives the power to be non-committal, to evade and equivocate.

4th. CUNNING.—A general fulness of the organ, which, unrestrained by sufficient moral power, leads to artfulness in little things, and systematic deception.

VERY LARGE.—Will seldom appear what you really are, liable often to equivocate and deceive. With deficient moral power, will be extremely given to double-dealing and great cunning; with large honesty, may be deep and only politic, yet unconsciously mysterious and lacking directness.

LARGE.—Will very seldom disclose any plan fully; are very anxious either to keep secrets or perhaps learn those of others; without sufficient conscientiousness, are often liable to unconsciously deceive; but with a strong moral sense of character, will show reserve, guardedness, and perhaps excessive prudence in speech.

FULL.—Can rather easily keep to yourself what you wish, but are not liable to be uniformly artful; are usually prudent and politic; with a warm temper, may sometimes speak out; but when calm, can easily control your thoughts and feelings. With large conscientiousness, will be honest; and when you do speak, will speak frankly.

AVERAGE.—Are neither artful nor very frank; with strong caution and judgment will conceal your thoughts, unless much excited; if temper is hasty, are quite liable occasionally to commit yourself in speaking.

MODERATE.—Are generally open and frank, not fond of concealment, and without reflection may often speak too quickly; if honesty is large, will be candid and straightforward in almost everything you do; are not fond of secretive people.

SMALL.—Are strongly disposed to speak out just what you think, and to act just what you feel; have no policy; are, glass-like, transparent, and, unless other faculties control you, may get into hot water with your extreme frankness. You should always think of consequences before a word is uttered in excitement; with large honesty, are incapable of deception.

To CULTIVATE.—Learn the act of thinking more and talking less; the judgment should especially be cultivated, for excessive frankness can only be properly regulated by the aid of reason. Avoid babbling; recollecting that the shallow, noisy brook is not so grand and noble as the deep river. Above all, avoid boring others with everything that happens to strike or please your fancy. Study your friends more, and recollect that while courtesy may compel them to listen to you, yet, unless you are very wise or witty, you are certain to be an intolerable bore. Speak quietly and slowly, and try to condense all that you say in a small compass, remembering that brevity is often the essence of wit, and that the age is too impatient to hear you out. If your temper is irritable, stimulate benevolence and kindness, so that what you would say in anger be either not said or robbed of its sting, remembering that pain is often caused not so much by what is spoken as by the venom which accompanies speech.

To RESTRAIN.—The opposite course must be pursued as the higher faculties may direct. Recollect that artifice, equivocation, and cunning are, in the eyes of all whose opinions are worth knowing, despicable. Note what society says of those whose frankness and openness of character render them invariably above suspicion. If your social faculties are defective, seek friends and open the portals of your heart to them. Avoid hinting, artfully insinuating, or winking; remember that *Mephistopheles* with his cunning is a character that no one loves. The successful restraint of this faculty demands the strongest exercise of conscientiousness, be it little or much. Honesty of speech is imperative—the revelation of all that should be revealed at a suitable time and place. No eavesdropping, no listening at keyholes, no stealthy creeping, no pretence and evasion must be practised, but a rigidly open demeanour, in which fearlessness, truth, and confidence in those around us are intimately blended.

CAUTIOUSNESS.

Prudence, watchfulness, sense of danger, and timidity. We give it four conditions :

1st. PRUDENCE.—Indicated by a fulness in the front part, and in giving a general sense of guardedness, forethought, and provision against difficulty.

2nd. SOLICITUDE.—A fuller development of the middle part, along with deficient hope and melancholic feelings, giving great anxiety as to results in regard to business, friends, &c.

3rd. TIMIDITY.—A fulness in the back part, along with defective combativeness, &c., giving the feeling of undefinable dread and a sense of faintheartedness.

4th. HESITATION.—A general fulness of the organ along with deficient firmness and self-esteem, giving the procrastinating and hesitating spirit.

VERY LARGE.—Are constantly liable to extreme hesitation and suffering from groundless fears; without a fair share of combativeness are likely to be frightened at shadows; if hope is deficient and nerves weak are certain to be in a constant state of misery and anxiety.

LARGE.—Are highly prudent, always on your guard against real or imaginary danger; without large firmness and force of character are often liable to be hesitating and timid ; with these large will be vigorous and forcible, but never rash or venturesome.

FULL.—Have a fair degree of prudence and forethought, and are only liable to fear danger when you really see it; with full combativeness and sense of character will often show pluck and spirit, with low combativeness and executiveness will often feel timid, but with a well-balanced brain are sufficiently prudent in all undertakings.

AVERAGE.—Have sufficient prudence, only if not well assisted by other faculties, if the judgment is weak, and the temperament excitable, will often be too rash ; with a strong will and good intellect, along with a calm nature, will seldom blunder, are likely to be neither timid nor rash.

MODERATE.—Will require to constantly exercise your judgment and power of self-restraint to keep you out of difficulty. By doing this you may go through the world in comparative safety, but your caution is otherwise too deficient for important enterprises. The cultivation of reason and will, will, however, do wonders.

SMALL.—Are constantly liable to act imprudently, to be reckless of consequences, and getting into hot water, never see danger; and while fearlessness may often carry you safely through, yet, without the restraining power of an excellent judgment, will have a long catalogue of blunders recorded against you.

To CULTIVATE.—Persons in whom this faculty is defective should constantly exercise their talents of planning and deliberation. All important enterprises should be well "thought out," and every minor detail faithfully attended to. You should give as far as possible a personal supervision to all your affairs, and trust nothing to chance ; but let the most remote item of your details of management be provided for ; remember what misery and ruin rash acts and words have done in all ages of the world. If in business, adhere strictly to the cash principle, even at the risk of offending. Make no promises unless there is a positive certainty that you can perform them. Avoid debt as you would avoid a nightmare. If you want advice, obtain it only from those of good judgment and experience ; and in your intercourse and dealings with all, try and rule your whole conduct by justice, reflection, and benevolence.

To RESTRAIN.—There are thousands of imaginary troubles, and those who are haunted by them should ascertain not only one, but all the causes. Some are constitutionally timid from weak nerves and weak digestion, and where these defects are accompanied by excessive caution, life is truly miserable. Hardening and strengthening the physical constitution is highly important, so as to give PHYSICAL courage. The faculty of HOPE may be defective, which is invariably an aggravation of timidity. If reason is defective, this should especially be encouraged, as a little philosophy is an excellent antidote to despair. You should keep a record of every instance in which your fears of trouble and danger are borne out by the facts, and you will probably find that in nine out of ten cases your alarm was perfectly groundless. Adopt the wise motto, "Sufficient unto the day is the evil thereof." Learn the great fact that human beings were originally designed to be happy, and that your megrims and fancies are whimsical and childish. You should act with decision; never keep putting off, as procrastination ruins thousands.

MISS SENTIMENTAL, or the unpractical Dreamer.—A contour denoting love of romance, poetry, and beauty, a longing for the unattainable, and for love and admiration.

THE UNSENTIMENTAL.— An Indian type denoting strong animal development and cunning, love of admiration, but no imagination; "of the earth earthy."

APPROBATIVENESS.

Sense of character, love of praise and popularity, desire to excel, sensitiveness and display. We give it four conditions:

1st. DESIRE FOR DISTINCTION.—A fulness in the inner part, adjoining self-esteem, giving the desire for superiority and excellence.

2nd. LOVE OF DISPLAY.—Fulness of the outer part, giving a love of dress and ornamentation in excess, *vanity.*

3rd. SENSE OF CHARACTER.—A fulness of the middle part, giving a sensitiveness to personal reputation and good name; a dread of ridicule and criticism.

4th. AFFECTATION.—A general fulness of the faculty, along with a defective intellect, and excessive desire to be agreeable, giving an artificial, servile, and shallow condition of the mind.

VERY LARGE.—Are excessively fond of approbation and praise; inclined to be extremely ceremonious; making displays; cannot endure patiently the smallest degree of criticism and censure.

LARGE.—Are inclined to set almost everything by character and reputation; cannot endure ridicule; with deficient conscientiousness, will be too fond of flattery; with large conscientiousness, would pride yourself on integrity and honour; with large identity, will be fond of display; and with deficient tact, are apt to praise yourself too much.

FULL.—Are rather fond of popularity and praise, but not excessively so; will enjoy it if it is obtained without much trouble; but you are capable of acting rather independently, especially if self-esteem and firmness are fully developed; with a good intellect and conscientiousness, will be much more proud of what you can do than of what you are.

AVERAGE.—Have hardly sufficient of this faculty to emulate and rival others for the sake of popularity; are very little disturbed by ordinary criticism and censure; and while you may enjoy praise, yet you are much more ruled in your doings and actions by other faculties than by the love of display or fame.

MODERATE.—Are likely to be too careless and reckless of popularity; are apt to feel and act just as you think, regardless of opinion.

SMALL.—Will care nothing for popularity and censure; will neither give praise nor care for receiving it.

To CULTIVATE.—As a deficiency of this faculty leads to a want of courtesy and the exhibition of those refining influences and amenities of social life, so its proper cultivation is most important. By giving a strong sense of character it often prevents crime, and deters many from mean and ignoble actions; along with agreeableness, it leads to politeness and affability toward others; and along with benevolence, is the prompting influence of thousands of beneficial and noble deeds of charity. Many persons receive the credit of being endowed with disinterested benevolence, whose kindnesses flow out from the expectation of pleasure in the gratification of this faculty. The systematic benevolence of the anonymous giver is only understood, *not* by its absence, but the innate satisfaction of doing good without display. You should learn that it is no weakness to honestly strive to earn fame and applause; the strong mind is strengthened and ennobled by it, while the weak and little mind only is injured or upset by receiving it. Learn to be quietly affable and courteous; say nothing rude or offensive; don't even say what you know to be true, when saying it will cause annoyance and harm to others; be the true *gentleman* or *lady* wherever you are, remembering that courtesy to all makes the wheels of life run smoothly.

To RESTRAIN.—Pursue the opposite course in part only, but make up your mind that you will fearlessly pursue the right regardless of frowns and censure. Your sensitiveness to criticism and opinion is likely to be a morbid influence that robs you of manly or womanly independence. Recollect the old philosopher who, when he was told that he was being accused and slandered by his enemies, simply replied "that he would live so that nobody should believe them." Above all, don't let the fear of failure deter you from trying to achieve. Do your best, and if laughed at, simply make up your mind to do better, and by excelling, laugh in turn: you should cultivate in yourself an heroic and individual spirit. Be only courteous, not vain or affected. If told of your faults, accept the reproof in a kindly spirit, and try and feel grateful to those who by honestly pointing out your defects would save you from derision and mortification ; in short, learn to be natural, unaffected, and easy, avoiding all boasting and self-praise, but with quiet ease and dignity proving to the world that a good conscience is your only monitor.

SELF-ESTEEM.

Self-love, dignity, desire to take responsibilities, appreciation of self. We give it four conditions :

1st. INDEPENDENCE.—Arising from a full development of the lower portion of the faculty, giving self-reliance and love of personal liberty.

2nd. SELF-LOVE.—A fulness in the central portion, giving self-appreciation and valuation of one's own works and sayings.

3rd. DIGNITY.—The upper portion adjoining firmness gives pride, manliness, the desire to lead and command the lofty-minded feeling.

4th. HAUTEUR.—A full development of the whole faculty, without the restraining influence of judgment and benevolence, gives a lofty contempt for others and the disposition to conceit.

VERY LARGE.—Have an unbounded degree of self-confidence, can endure no restraint, and are inclined to be very haughty and imperious ; unless judgment and friendship are strong can never take advice.

LARGE.—Are high-minded and independent, self-confident and dignified, strongly inclined to be your own master and to assume responsibilities ; cannot brook restraint or descend to do little things ; without good judgment may often appear conceited to others ; with large approbativeness are likely to be very ambitious and aspiring.

FULL.—Are endowed with a good share of self-respect ; usually are rather self-confident, especially if you have had experience ; will occasionally hesitate, but if your will and energy are strong, you will not be wanting in self-reliance ; would only appear conceited from a deficient judgment ; with an otherwise well-balanced brain have a proper degree of self-esteem.

AVERAGE.—Have only a fair share of confidence, will require a thorough training and education to render you self-reliant ; with approbativeness large, may be ambitious and appear self-confident to others, but do not always feel it ; if caution is large and combativeness is deficient, will feel the need of much experience and culture to give sufficient confidence.

MODERATE.—Are deficient of self-reliance and dignity, and unless you carefully watch yourself may be often tempted to do and say what is beneath you, and so fail to command the respect of others ; with large approbativeness, are apt to be morbidly sensitive: with approbativeness small, are too liable to let yourself down by associating with inferiors ; and if the passions are strong, may from want of pride be led into trouble: are constantly liable to undervalue yourself.

SMALL.—Have no dignity or sense of individual pride of character ; with large approbativeness may be morbidly bashful : you should remember that you are constantly liable to be too trifling and insignificant.

To CULTIVATE.—The improvement of this faculty can only be successfully accomplished by the systematic and persistent cultivation of other powers. To be conceited and assuming without mental resources and knowledge is the height of foolishness ; and in the improvement of self-esteem you must recollect that in all rightly-constituted minds a general enlargement and culture of all the mental powers are necessary. Never go into company empty-headed. Feel that you know something important and useful, even if you never mention it ; for the consciousness of your resources will promote a calm confidence, as the man of business with outstanding debts feels easy and confident with a good balance at his bankers. You should not only learn, but talk about what you do learn, and as you succeed in interesting others you give assurance to yourself. Push quietly forward in company or in public ; attend debates, assemblies ; read in public, sing or speak in public, and don't be mortified at failure, but persevere till what you can do in private in your own quiet room can be done as easily before hundreds of listeners. Do all that you attempt without arrogance or pomposity, but do it feeling that it is the right thing for you to do; and in all your associations strive to select those as companions who are educated and dignified, so that their example will be a continual stimulus to exertion.

To RESTRAIN.—To do this it is necessary to recollect that true great ness belongs most to *modest, humility*, not to presumption and egotism. No truly great man is conceited. Along with conceit an individual may be brilliant and clever, but his conceit is a positive weakness that continually exposes him to ridicule. You should especially study the science of character, and all the sciences that explain man, as you would then learn " scientifically " that thousands in the world are equal or perhaps superior to yourself. Think of *King Canute* on the sea shore, and his rebuke to his flatterers. If you feel your dignity offended by others, ask yourself the reason of it, and you will probably discover the real cause to be some vanity or weakness of your own; for you must recollect that the world is armed against the proud and overbearing individual who foolishly assumes superiority, and whatever homage he may receive from others will be grudgingly yielded, and without eminent and brilliant talents he will invariably be regarded with scorn and contempt.

WELLINGTON.—Face indicates great kindness, honesty, moral courage—not physical; large order and system, prudence, decision, and exactness; a physiognomy to win and retain confidence; the shrewd and clear-headed warrior.

NAPOLEON I., the man of destiny.—Face indicates pre-eminent genius, towering ambition, and great selfishness; great secretiveness, coldness, will, decision, along with but little sympathy; a powerful nature, but conflicting in greatness and littleness.

MORAL AND RELIGIOUS SENTIMENTS.

FIRMNESS.

Power of will, fixedness of purpose, positiveness, and unyielding tenacity. We give it four conditions:

1st. POWER OF WILL.—Given chiefly by development of the lower part, and implies the power to decide quickly, to be positive and prompt in decision.

2nd. STABILITY.—A full development of the middle portion gives steadiness and solidity of opinion.

3rd. PERSEVERANCE.—The front part gives the desire to finish whatever is undertaken.

4th. STUBBORNNESS.—A general fulness of the organ, along with a positive and unyielding temperament, deficient agreeableness and benevolence, causes dogmatism and the stubborn disposition.

VERY LARGE.—Are exceedingly wilful and unchangeable, without the modifying influences of other faculties are certain to be disagreeably stubborn; like the statutes of the Medes and Persians—unalterable. Unless benevolence and sociability are large, are liable to be offensively dogmatic and tenacious.

LARGE.—Are generally as firm as the enduring rock, fond of having your own way, and with full executiveness are very persistent; with large CONTINUITY, will seldom or never give up anything you undertake; are only strengthened by opposition, but yet with good reasoning faculties and benevolence will not appear stubborn or unreasonable to others; without these, are certain to be stubborn.

FULL.—You have perseverance and will enough for ordinary occasions, but, unless continuity and executiveness are fully developed will sometimes yield under trying influences; with a well-balanced brain, would have sufficient will for all ordinary situations in life; are not likely to be either fickle or stubborn.

AVERAGE.—Have a fair degree of decision, but are not persistent and firm enough for positions requiring great will-power; with executiveness and continuity full or large may be energetic and persevering, but you lack the stubborn tenacity that yields not even in the long and strong pull.

MODERATE.—Are decidedly too weak in fixity of purpose, and if caution is large will often suffer from indecision; with small continuity, are liable to be quite fickle and changeable.

SMALL.—Are quite too vacillating, and if timid will be in a constant fever of indecision; will require the aid of large continuity and strong executiveness to succeed in anything worth achieving.

To CULTIVATE.—To those who are deficient of will, the study of biography, of the lives of eminent and successful men, is highly important, recollecting that no fickle and changeable individual has ever achieved anything worth remembering. There is never any necessity of being unreasonably stubborn. Knowing what to do, laying out a plan by which to do it, and then never losing sight of the project till it is triumphantly accomplished. If you are right be firm, and recollect that an unflinching and persistent will, acting on the right side, will extort admiration and respect even from enemies. To promote this organ it is necessary to have a definite and settled purpose in life, some great design which can be accomplished only by systematical application, and every accessory of action brought to bear in its achievement. You should learn that the "*I can't*" is a childish confession of incompetence. Whatever is worthy to be done, that do, and create in yourself the knowledge and power to do it. Never allow circumstances to dominate your will, but make circumstances and conditions your slaves. Recollect the heroic Nelson, when signalled to retreat from the battle, putting the glass to his blind eye, and declaring that he did not see the signal, and so fought on and won. In short, be quietly but determinedly firm.

To RESTRAIN.—To do this, first ascertain how you personally stand in relation to others. Ask yourself if it is wise and noble to imitate and emulate the donkey, instead of yielding gracefully when you are in the wrong, or quietly abandoning a position in which you can be of no use to yourself or others. The cultivation of benevolence and charity is important, as an extremely stubborn will blinds one to the better qualities of those with whom they even temporarily disagree. Don't be always wishing to give tit for tat. As you are not omniscient, you are likely to be in the wrong; and if you know you are in the right, be satisfied with it, and let your quiet tact and affability alone give you the victory.

CONSCIENTIOUSNESS.

Sense of justice, equity, disposition to be right and to do right. We give it four conditions :

1st. CIRCUMSPECTION.—Arising from the development of the outer portion, giving consistency of life and character, and love of propriety.

2nd. INTEGRITY.—Fulness of the middle part, giving a sense of faithfulness to engagements, and general truthfulness.

3rd. JUSTICE.—Fulness of the upper part, adjoining firmness, giving a sense of moral obligation and of religious duty.

4th. SELF-ACCUSATION.—A general activity of the faculty, along with a high moral tone and defective hope, giving a sense of unworthiness, guilt, and inefficiency.

VERY LARGE.—Are scrupulously exact in matters of right, puritanical in conscience, likely to be always condemning yourself and repenting of imaginary transgressions. With deficient hope and strong religious sense, are likely to be very morbid in matters of duty.

LARGE.—Are honest at heart, with a high degree of natural rectitude of purpose. With moderate selfish faculties only, are extremely honest in motive, and grateful to those who do you a kindness. Are not apt to consult expediency or knowingly do wrong, except under extraordinary pressure. With equally large selfish faculties will feel occasional temptation, though you may never yield to it.

FULL.—Will strive to do right, and with good moral qualities, and not strong, selfish faculties, may easily live an honest, upright life; but without otherwise good moral support will be likely to yield to temptation through besetting sins, and then experience remorse for doing so. With large self-esteem and approbativeness are likely to be honest, partly for the sake of maintaining your good name.

AVERAGE.—Have a fair degree of right intentions, but their influence is likely to be too limited, unless with a high degree of moral and religious influence the organ is strictly controlled. If selfishness is deficient, may not experience a deficiency of conscience, yet are liable to waive certain duties and obligations that may seriously affect yourself or others.

MODERATE.—Have some regard for duty and honesty, but are quite apt to temporize with principle, apt to justify yourself, and are not so scrupulous as you should be; may get through the world fairly, but your reputation will largely depend on the controlling power of other faculties, and on circumstances.

SMALL.—Have few conscientious scruples, constantly liable to be negligent of the stern behests of right and duty, and are likely only to be honest under compulsion.

TO CULTIVATE.—In order to do this successfully constant self-denial and a strong will are demanded—perpetual resistance to any and every temptation that besets you ; as in every well-regulated society nothing is so disastrous to reputation as a dishonest action, so there is nothing that inspires confidence like unswerving integrity. Do not be honest because "honesty is the best policy," that view is degrading and unmanly ; be honest from simple honesty ; be too proud and noble to be otherwise. Always before speaking or acting think of what the reacting influence is going to be upon yourself in placing you on a higher or lower place in your own estimation, and reflect that every act of insincerity and weakness makes a bigger platform for other faults to crowd upon. In cultivating this faculty in children, example is indispensable. What is promised should be strictly performed. Pampering and pacifying them with lies should be regarded as a crime or dreadful blunder; for children are clever imitators, and if they have an untruthful copy their plastic natures are unconsciously modeled by it, and parents often in harshness degrade their children into habitual dishonesty by brutally punishing them for being endowed with inherited faults, and which are only capable of being overcome by appealing constantly to their affections and judgment.

To RESTRAIN.—This is essentially necessary when the whole temperament is morbid, the nerves weak, and the individual is subject to melancholia. Many persons suffer from morbid conscientiousness from over religious excitement, being afflicted with the idea that they have committed unpardonable sins that can never be condoned. Excessive conscientiousness is occasionally shown in matters of business; in undervaluing ourselves and what we do we give far more than value received, and are injured by the selfishness of those not over scrupulous. If you are morbidly conscientious, you should seek the advice of some intelligent and honourable friend, and learn from them how to act. If you fancy yourself to be a great sinner, without a hope of pardon, recollect that no divine law can exact from you what you are morally incapable of giving, and that such feelings amount only to a conscientious superstition ; and also remember, when inclined to be severe on the peccadilloes and shortcomings of others, that justice must always be tempered with mercy and charity.

HOPE.

Expectation and anticipation, buoyancy and cheerfulness, sense of immortality.   We give it four conditions :

1st. SPECULATION.—Arising from the lower part of the organ, which along with a trading disposition gives enterprise, the inclination to venture and run risks.

2nd. HOPE PRESENT.—The middle part along with an otherwise happy disposition gives the anticipation and desire for success as connected with this life.

3rd. HOPE FUTURE.—Fulness of the upper part along with spirituality gives the sense of immortality or consciousness of another life.

4th. EXAGGERATION.—A fulness of the front part adjoining marvellousness unrestrained by reflection gives a tendency to exaggerate and magnify.

VERY LARGE.—Have unbounded hopes, and are constantly building castles in the air ; with deficient continuity will have numberless irons in the fire ; are liable to exaggerate and suffer severe but temporary disappointment from expecting too much.

LARGE.—Have a vivid anticipation of future results, expect great things, and if disappointed will still hope on ; with a sanguine temperament will be as buoyant as a cork, with an impulsive nature are quite likely to be rash in making promises and professions, with good judgment and prudence are sure to be both happy and successful, though you are liable to suffer occasionally the reactionary disappointment of hoping for too much.

FULL.—Are generally quite sanguine, yet not too much so ; with an ordinarily good judgment will realise about what you expect; are occasionally elated, but if caution is large are not inclined to venture too far ; if brain is otherwise well-balanced and health good, will have an equanimity of cheerfulness.

AVERAGE.—Have hope enough for ordinary enterprises along with a sanguine temperament, but too little for a melancholic one ; if health is defective and caution large strive to improve one and restrain the other, are rather likely to see the darker side.

MODERATE.—Are constantly liable to hope for less than you get, and will often succeed better than you think you are going to do ; are prone to despond, and with large caution are certain to be always bridging your difficulties before you reach them.

SMALL.—Are low-spirited, constantly liable to say *I can't*, very easily discouraged, and magnify evil; with defective health and large timidity are certain to be labouring under constant depression and gloominess; with a good constitution and deficient caution may not suffer severely yet have little or no enterprise.

To CULTIVATE.—The cultivation of this faculty is important for two reasons—improvement of health and promoting enterprise. It is a very sad condition to be hopeless, and when the temperament is gloomy and melancholie, added to low hope, life becomes a positive burden; if health is deficient you must first use every means for its restoration, as a healthy body promotes a healthy condition of the mind. You must as far as possible rid yourself of all dispensable cares and business perplexities, undertaking no responsibilities likely to involve anxiety. You should then endeavour to create something to hope for, study the philosophy of life and how to act in order to realise solid success. Avoid all gloomy associations, all who have elongated visage and fretful natures, and then, after studying the real causes of your own morbid fancies, invoke every means to remove those causes, and remember that morbid despondency is unmanly, unwomanly, and unhealthy; that the divine creator made a beautiful world full of gladdening influences if we only render ourselves receptive to them, and that there is no desert without an oasis, no cloud without a silver lining.

To RESTRAIN.—This is necessary where hope leads to exaggeration, over-speculation, gambling, over-promising, and building so many air castles that we are in a constant whirl of anticipation and disappointment. You should avoid all promises where calm judgment does not see the direct way to their practical performance; should avoid all lending and borrowing money, all running in debt, subtract a large percentage from your buoyant anticipations, and make up your mind to be satisfied with half the success you desire. If your temperament is highly sensitive, recollect that your unbounded hope may be a great source of misery to you, as you are apt to paint your future in such glowing colours that the realisation will often turn out a disappointing and wretched daub; in short, depend on plodding industry and careful forethought, keeping your wings of imagination clipped so that you may not be tempted to soar too high above the stern and solid realities of the every-day world.

SPIRITUALITY OR MARVELLOUSNESS.

Belief in and love of the wonderful and supernatural; credulity; trust in the unseen and in providence. We give it four conditions:

1st. WONDER.—The lower part gives a sense of the novel and marvellous, a disposition to onlarge upon and magnify.

2nd. CREDULITY.—The middle part gives a trust in the unseen, unproved, and unreal, a sense of simple belief.

3rd. INVESTIGATION.—The front part acting with intellect gives a love of searching in order to harmonize the unknown with the known.

4th.—SUPERSTITION.—The back part, in conjunction with hope and reverence and with deficient reason, gives blind faith, the tendency to believe in ghosts and supernatural visitations.

VERY LARGE.—Are inclined to be excessively superstitious, to believe blindly without judgment; with large reason will be fond of investigating all things wonderful.

LARGE.—Are strongly inclined to believe in the supernatural and unreal; will often ponder over the mysterious and wonderful; with a good intellect are not likely to be superstitious, yet are quite likely to have your judgment more or less controlled by a sense of the spiritual or marvellous; may or may not believe in ghosts, dreams, &c., as this is largely a matter of training and education, yet the size of the faculty must largely influence you.

FULL.—Are quite open to conviction with an ordinary good judgment; may be credulous with the bias of your education, but will only be superstitious with a weak judgment; if reasoning powers are strong, are not likely to be at all superstitious.

AVERAGE.—May believe some in forewarnings and the wonderful, but with age and experience are certain to become more incredulous and doubting; with a weak faculty of reason may be strongly biased by education; with a strong intellect would strive to account for everything by natural causes.

MODERATE.—Are not liable to believe much that cannot be accounted for by good evidence; may be open to conviction by tangible demonstration, but not otherwise; are inclined to be incredulous, and shake off much that you believed in childhood.

SMALL.—Are convinced only with great difficulty; are distrustful of the truth of all things unseen and mysterious; with a strong intellect have a tendency to decided scepticism, and believe nothing till you can demonstrate it.

CHARLOTTE CORDAY, the heroine of the French revolution, who killed *Marat* in order to save France.—A face indicating great courage and devotion.

AN ALBANIAN WOMAN.—Showing coarseness, vigour, voluptuality, and love of sensuous gratification, combined with general intelligence; deficient spirituality.

To CULTIVATE.—The proper cultivation of this faculty is important for many reasons; it serves to endow the mind with a power of instinctive belief in that which pure reason can never account for; and apart from religious belief the world of nature itself is full of grand and sublime mysteries, which to even perceive and feel without the aid of reason has an elevating and refining tendency. There is no need of ghostly communication, or of clinging to any baseless tradition. There is a world of mystery around us that demands an inquisitive desire on the part of the human mind, and when reason and intellect can go no farther this faculty instinctively accepts the profound and unreasoned mystery lying beyond as a mighty truth. You must recollect that to understand spiritual laws and forces it requires more than reason; the moral faculties perceive spiritual things as causality perceives causes, or comparison perceives analogies, and it is no evidence of a strong mind to reject what intellect alone cannot understand; and to properly cultivate this faculty you should try to realise the operation of beneficent and unseen principles, the wonders and mysteries of human life, the incomprehensible wisdom displayed throughout the universe, and never deny the wonderful and mysterious because you cannot understand them. You are finite, while God and the universe are infinite, and your reason may deceive you as it has deceived the wise men of all ages.

To RESTRAIN.—To a great extent the opposite course must be pursued ; learn that there is a primary cause for all that you do not understand ; recollect that superstition properly belongs only to a dark age, that it is a morbid or diseased condition of this part of the brain ; and think of what science has done with the superstition of the middle ages. You should constantly exercise your judgment and reason, and learn that ghosts and spectres are always the creations of a disordered fancy ; be credulous only of ascertained and positive truth. What seems incredible do not put it on the shelf, but unravel it by piecemeal, or till you satisfy yourself that your intellect is only lacking sufficient strength to tear the whole fabric of delusion to fragments.

VENERATION.

Adoration, worship, respect, and reverence for Deity, for age, and antiquity. We give it four divisions :

1st. RESPECT FOR SUPERIORS.— The front part adjoining benevolence leads to great deference to and regard for superiors and for the aged.

2nd. DESIRE TO WORSHIP.—In the middle part of the organ we have the tendency to worship, to feel awe, and a sense of adoration.

3rd. REVERENCE TO DEITY.—The back part of the organ gives a sense of reverence toward the Supreme Being.

4th. IDOLATRY.—Arising from a general fulness of the faculty in conjunction with a moderate intellect, and an impressible temperament gives a tendency to idolize and create objects for worship.

VERY LARGE.—Have an extreme reverence for everything appertaining to sacred and divine things. If religious will be excessively devotional, with other large moral faculties, will be pre-eminent for piety and heart-felt devotion.

LARGE.—Are strongly inclined to the devotional spirit, are usually respectful and reverential ; with deficient self-esteem will treat superiors with marked deference ; with strong faith and belief are capable of a high degree of devotional piety.

FULL.—Are capable of a considerable degree of religious devotion and reverence, but it is modified by other prominent faculties ; are usually respectful, but not invariably or habitually serious, and with other moral powers large will show no deficiency of a devotional spirit : are not likely to be a great respecter of persons.

AVERAGE.—Have only a fair share of devotional feeling, and if a religious worshipper are more influenced by other faculties than that of pure reverence. With large conscientiousness, will be honest in belief ; with large benevolence, charitable : with large hope, may be enthusiastic ; but you lack in the highest feelings of devotion.

MODERATE.—Are apt to disregard creeds and the devotional phases of religion. With large intellectual powers, may be sceptical. May with other well-developed moral faculties be earnest and honest, but are strongly inclined to place religion in other things than in devotional worship. Not likely to be sufficiently respectful to age.

SMALL.—Have little or no real respect for any kind of religious worship : will not understand the meaning of devotion ; and unless guided by other strong moral qualities, are likely to scoff at all respect or reverence paid to divine things, or to old age.

To CULTIVATE.—To do this it is necessary to be convinced of the absolute importance of habitual respect paid to whatever is true and good. You must remember that the "devotional" is a refining and elevating influence, inciting us not only to render homage where homage is due, but constantly leading us to aspire more toward that which we should reverence and worship. No matter what others believe, or you disbelieve, a proper degree of respect should be conceded to their views ; and if you cannot worship what ten persons or millions of human beings worship, you should learn to reverence something in accordance with your highest judgment, and you must learn that a proper respect for the opinions of others is one form of reverence. To scoff at the honest convictions of others shows a want of nobleness—a certain amount of depravity ; and you must also recollect that a full development and exercise of this faculty is necessary to comprehend spiritual things and the character of the Divine Being ; for without reverence your intellect is likely to mislead you.

To RESTRAIN.—This is essential when by extreme reverence you are servile and slavish toward those in higher rank or wealthier position. You should recollect that when homage is paid to an unworthy object, it is an idolatrous and abject condition of mind, and that tyranny, slavery, and villainy are too often upheld by cringing, debasing servitude. You should reverence Deity, truth, and old age ; but bend and cringe to nothing which is unworthy of homage. Try and avoid being reverential toward old institutions and old things merely because they are old. The new that has grown up on their ruins may be a thousand times more worthy your respect. Avoid antiquarian hobbies, or slaving your mind in the search for ancient rubbish. Seek for and find more intelligent sources of adoration in that not merely sanctified by antiquity. Above all, cultivate an intelligent appreciation, not a blind worship, of anything. Remember that even the Divine Creator would not exact idolatrous homage, but would demand your adoration only so far as it is consistent with your intelligent appreciation of His character and bounties.

BENEVOLENCE.

Liberality, sympathy, and the desire to do good. We give it four conditions :

1st. SYMPATHY.—The development of the back part gives an interest in the success and welfare of others, tenderness and kindness of feeling.

2nd. LIBERALITY.—Fulness in the middle part gives the disposition to aid others by giving or lending apart from any special sympathetic feeling.

3rd. PHILANTHROPY.—The front part gives a regard for general welfare ; to assist in great moral, educational, or religious enterprises ; often aided by approbativeness.

4th. RELIEF OF NECESSITY.—An equal development of the faculty, along with large conscientiousness ; judgment and caution gives the disposition only to relieve special and deserving cases from a sense of duty.

VERY LARGE.—Are inclined to do all the good in your power and be profusely liberal ; without caution large, would be reckless in giving ; with small acquisitiveness, will regard property only as a means of doing good : are quite likely to be too much the *Father Bountiful*.

LARGE.—Are naturally kind-hearted and benevolent, disposed to give bountifully unless restrained by other powers ; with small or weak selfish faculties would harm yourself by your sympathy for others ; with large acquisitiveness would accumulate money, and then dispense it freely ; with large caution and domestic faculties would be liberal, but would make CHARITY begin at home.

FULL.—Have a fair share of sympathetic feeling, and willingly do good where it lies fairly in your power, but are not likely to be profuse; with deficient selfish faculties will think much of the benefits and interests of those around you; but with large caution and strong acquisitiveness would be almost entirely influenced by other considerations in giving, perhaps from friendship or religious duty.

AVERAGE.—Have a rather kind fellow-feeling, but not much spontaneous and active benevolence; with large friendship would assist friends; with large conscientiousness and religious feeling would give chiefly from a sense of moral obligation.

MODERATE.—Are sympathetic and benevolent only to a limited degree; if selfish faculties are large will think of self in everything; with large friendship would be kind to friends, but have too little sympathy and liberality, and should promote it.

SMALL.—Are narrow-minded and mean; have so little sympathy and benevolence that you are likely to be quite deaf to the cry of distress.

GEORGE FRANCIS TRAIN, the ambitious Fanatic.—The contour exhibits great enterprise and daring, unscrupulous audacity, vigour, and coarseness, along with unbounded self-reliance; a boaster and demagogue; not much benevolence.

ROWLAND HILL, the originator of the Penny Post, the far-seeing reformer.—A face indicating great earnestness, projecting power, sympathy, and geniality, along with sensitiveness and high quality of organization; large benevolence.

To CULTIVATE.—The improvement of this faculty is of the highest importance; it is the foundation of all charity; and without charity human society would have but few attractions. The proper cultivation of benevolence would be to do all the good that lies in our power; not lavish profusion in giving, but practical and genuine sympathy running through the whole current of life. You may be prayerful, honest, believing, consistent in worldly-accepted Christianity, and yet sordid, narrow-minded, unmerciful, and intolerant. All these are lessened or destroyed by benevolence. It is the true law of love, and comprises the gist of that important injunction, " *Do unto others as ye would that others should do unto you.*" You should also recollect that success in life largely depends on the constant manifestation of benevolence. Those who are habitually kind are never without friends, and many otherwise serious faults are condoned or overlooked, which, if combined with a sordid and selfish spirit, would blast all hopes of advancement; and, though it is not the highest benevolence because of its policy, it is infinitely better than its absence. You should learn practically "that it is more blessed to give than to receive."

To RESTRAIN.—This is necessary where foolish and lavish generosity injures others, and is detrimental to ourselves. You should learn that charity properly begins at home, and that kindnesses, to be useful, must be directed with both intelligence and honesty, as it is often dishonest to ourselves to be over-liberal. You should be rigidly systematic in exacting the return of everything which properly belongs to you. Don't lend and forget. Do not give without first ascertaining that your gifts are required and acceptable; and do not involve yourself with the acceptance of obligations that you will feel compelled to be always paying. A man was once drowning; an impecunious individual, being a good swimmer, rescued him. He was liberally rewarded; but the rescued man was incessantly dogged by his rescuer for assistance. "Saved your life, you know," was the ground of the appeal. At last, after gifts innumerable, the patience of the rescued man was exhausted, and, throwing the other an additional sovereign, exclaimed, "There! if you ever see me drowning again, let me drown; for I am tired of being saved."

Bishop FRASER, the wide-awake, practical man of the world.—Inventive, clear-headed, determined, and executive.

Miss D——.—Easy-going, artistic, imitative, but no powers of invention or originality.

CONSTRUCTIVENESS.

Contrivance, ingenuity, and planning talent, applied either to business, to mechanics, art, literature, or music. It has four conditions:

1st. MANUAL DEXTERITY.—The lower and back portion gives the power to work with ease and dispatch—a sense of physical handiness.

2nd. CONTRIVANCE.—The middle portion gives the sense of mechanical contrivance, to suggest improvements, and the desire to use tools.

D

3rd. INVENTION.—The front portion adjoining intellect gives the desire to originate and invent—to apply principles.

4th. VERBAL CONSTRUCTION.—The top portion adjoining ideality gives the power of verbal arrangement and method, as in poetry, oratory, composition, &c.

VERY LARGE.—Have a great natural power of construction, an incessant desire to plan, with large perceptive organs; are capable of being a mechanician of the first order; with large literary abilities, would be pre-eminent in power of verbal arrangement.

LARGE.—Will show great natural powers of planning and devising ways and means; with *form* and *size* large, would excel in mechanics; with large, reflective, and perceptive powers, would be excellent at invention; are disposed to be mechanical and constructive in everything you do.

FULL.—Have a good degree of ingenuity, yet no great natural talent; with large imitative and perceptive powers, would excel as a practical worker or copyist; can suggest improvements, and plan to good advantage, yet your mechanical skill will depend on other faculties : are not highly original.

AVERAGE.—Have a fair degree of talent for devising and planning; will frequently have to depend on the plans of others ; may be a good copyist or finisher in what you do, but are not original or ingenious mechanically.

MODERATE.—Are deficient of constructive power, and if perceptive powers are weak, would be rather blundering in using tools ; with large form, size, imitation, may copy readily and correctly, but cannot depend on any success on original construction.

SMALL.—Are likely to be quite awkward and bungling in using tools, as applied to any mechanical employment ; when devising and originating are required, may copy fairly or with large physical perception might succeed as a workman, but without these are a complete blunderer.

To CULTIVATE.—As thousands fail, not from lack of industry or perseverance, but from want of ingenuity, so it is important in the cultivation of this faculty that everything attempted should be based on some definite plan. This *faculty*, applying as it does to our every performance in life, gives business and mechanical foresight. He who has it largely developed sees clearly the application of all that he does to-day to the exigencies of to-morrow. He is seldom or never taken by surprise, for he has perhaps "prearranged" the work of months or years; along with order and calculation it gives system, punctuality, and method, and is equally necessary to the orator or poet as to the skilled workman. Many good workmen are deficient of it, but they are men of routine, always working in a groove, and never succeed when new ideas are demanded. By always laying out to-day the work of to-morrow ; by arranging, prearranging, doing all by method and system, avoiding servility of imitation, your chances of independence and success will be largely increased.

To RESTRAIN.—This is essential where there are such a succession of plans presenting themselves to the mind, that too many things are attempted and impracticable schemes set in motion. The "perpetual motion" mania "belongs to the excessive action of this faculty," not properly regulated by that *reason* "that suggested the law of gravitation." It is also necessary to restrain it when valuable time is lost by being absorbed with the patent-right mania. Along with large hope, it puts an endless number of irons in the fire ; and when continuity is also deficient, it cuts all the efforts of life into broken fragments ; everything tried, but nothing finally accomplished. You should study principles of action, and attempt nothing new till you have completed the old. Take the plan that seems to your calm judgment the most feasible, and pursue it to finality, remembering that between two stools thousands fall to the ground.

Tom Faed, R.A.—An artist face indicating great perception and sense of physical harmony, the power to reproduce touching and pathetic scenes from nature, an intense and vigorous character, refinement and power blended, strong friendship, ideality, &c.

Miall, M.P., the Reformer, writer, and thinker.—A face indicating intense thought, continuity, and perseverance (reflection preponderating over perception), great mental vigour, and fine quality, along with high moral powers.

IDEALITY.

The poetical feeling, sense of refinement, perfection, and beauty. We give it four conditions :

1st. Imagination.—The back part adjoining sublimity gives the power to embellish and magnify, to fully represent by imagery what the mind feels.

2nd. Refinement.—The middle part gives general polish and taste, the feeling of poetic sympathy, and love of style and beauty in dress, manners, &c.

3rd. Love of Perfection.—The front part adjoining intellect gives the desire to realize the highest perfection in character, in art, literature, music, or mechanism.

4th. Fastidiousness.—A general fulness of the upper part of the faculty, along with high sensitiveness, gives the feeling of uncongeniality to others in tastes, habits, and pursuits, frequently a morbid refinement.

Very Large.—Have an intense desire for perfection, and cannot tolerate the slightest deviation from it; with high organic quality will be fastidious and squeamish, and without good intellectual power would be erratic, visionary, and highly impractical; with other powers suitable have the foundation for the highest order of poetry, &c.

Large.—Have a lively imagination, and a strong sense of the beautiful and perfect in nature, art, or oratory ; and with equally good intellectual power will be often brilliant and versatile in your ideas; will keenly desire perfection in everything, yet with deficient perception are sure to be impractical ; with large form and colour would delight in flowers and artistical productions, or with strong mechanical faculties would excel in the higher branches of art and mechanism.

Full.—Have a fair degree of refinement, and at times will feel strongly the sense of poetry and enthusiasm, but are likely to be more practical than imagina-

D 2

tive; with a fine quality of organisation have sufficient taste and refinement in whatever you are otherwise qualified to do.

AVERAGE.—Are generally practical and everydaylike, not visionary or disposed to much imagination; may feel poetry, but are not metaphorical; with otherwise good practical talents are not likely to soar far above mother earth; with a fine *organic tone* may, however, show sufficient taste in whatever you attempt.

MODERATE.—Are too deficient of imagination to realize any success in poetical imagery, and if your organization otherwise is coarse are liable to fall into grossness and vulgarisms; with a good intellect and moral power may show no special want of refinement and ideality of feeling.

SMALL.—Are decidedly lacking in taste and refinement, intensely practical and commonplace in manners and feeling, and unless organic quality is tolerably high are apt to neglect and despise everything tending to refinement.

TO CULTIVATE.—In doing this it is first necessary to understand the true value of culture in the elevation and refinement of character. Think of what the world would be without its infinite and varied beauties impressing themselves on the imagination, and also what social life would be if all the graces and amenities given by this faculty were taken out of it. You should recollect that elegance of dress and manners are essential to civilization, that human existence is only valuable to ourselves and the world in proportion as we aspire to perfection, that beauty is as useful as plainness, and that to sneer at elegance and refining influences shows a positive weakness of understanding and lowness of feeling. There is no need of being artificial, vain, or visionary; but you should learn that poetry, painting, eloquence, refined manners, and dress are unfading charms with which the world is becoming more acquainted. Avoid vulgarity of language, read works of imagination, study flowers and botany, hang your walls with whatever is beautiful to the eye, hear the most eloquent preachers and speakers, and learn to appreciate the beautiful and true everywhere.

TO RESTRAIN.—This is essential where it leads to artificiality of life and character and bombastic exaggeration of speech. You should especially avoid all fastidiousness and squeamishness in regard to that which is honest and true, "but plain," recollecting that while the cabbage is not nearly so beautiful as the rose it is of far greater practical value. You must recollect that dress does not constitute the man or woman, and that great gentility may be closely allied to great self-imposed deception, and to be conventional is to be servile. You should learn that the gewgaws of fashion are only beautiful in proportion as they are subordinate to the person. Speak plainly, without mincing and selecting "rosewater" sentences; be earnest, direct, and practical, making efficiency, vigour, brevity, and simplicity the faithful guides of every action.

SUBLIMITY.

Sense of the vast and magnificent, of the endless, sublime, and infinite. We give it three conditions:

1st. LOVE OF GRANDEUR.—The front part adjoining ideality gives a love of scenery, of the picturesque and grand in nature.

2nd. LOVE OF THE SUBLIME.—The back part gives a sense of the wild, terrific, and extravagant.

3rd. EXPANSIVENESS.—The middle part gives a sense of the vast, endless, infinite, as in astronomy, space, &c.

VERY LARGE.—Are a passionate admirer of the wild and romantic in nature, and are highly capable of realizing the boundlessness of space, the grandeur and sublimity of natural phenomena, as shown in lightning and thunder and the commotion of the elements.

LARGE.—Are a keen admirer of the grand and terrific in nature; love a grand prospect and mountain scenery; and if a traveller, would never weary while nature entertained you with her varied and mighty movements and her rugged and lofty peaks.

FULL.—Will admire and enjoy mountain scenery, thunder and lightning, tolerably well, but are not excessively enraptured; with a large intellect and a practical temperament would appreciate without enthusiasm.

AVERAGE.—Are not a lover of the sublime and vast; may fairly appreciate it, but will let other matters arrest your attention in preference; without ideality fully developed would be quite practical.

MODERATE.—Are deficient of the sense of the sublime, are not awe-struck at the sublimity and grandour of the universe, and without ideality would be quite prosaic and practical.

SMALL.—Have little or no sense of the grand and infinite as displayed in nature, and if marvellousness and ideality are small will go through life with a muck-rake, seeing no grandeur or beauty anywhere.

To CULTIVATE.—The most effectual methods are, first, travelling if possible ; or if this is *not* practicable, constant and systematic study by the aid of the telescope and microscope. You should live if possible in a rugged mountain region, as those who inhabit such regions—as the Scotch and Swiss—have this faculty highly developed. A crowded, busy city life is unfavourable to its cultivation ; solitude, communion with nature, reading (if the intellect can appreciate them) Milton, parts of Shakespeare and Byron, the Psalms, the poems of Ossian, and all subjects treating poetically on astronomy or on the infinite nature and works of the divine Creator.

To RESTRAIN.—To do this it is necessary to promote a practical earthly feeling, the vast and boundless should be left to take care of itself, and you should shut out resolutely all engrossing contemplation of them ; should live in the midst of practical, every-day people who are more inclined to go down with the spade than up with a balloon ; the real and useful should take precedence in all your thoughts, and you should avoid all solitude, staying at home ; or, if you travel, go on business and attend to your business ; talk prose, keep a ledger, learn to be commonplace and realistic, keep your wings clipped, try and become clever in the ordinary chit-chat of society, and you may soon become clever enough to regard a fashionable coterie as infinitely more interesting than the whole universe.

IMITATION.

The ability to copy and pattern from others ; to mimic and imitate what we see or hear. We give it four conditions :

1st. MIMICRY.—The front part adjoining mirthfulness gives the power to act as others act, to represent whatever is ludicrous or peculiar.

2nd. ASSIMILATION TO OTHERS.—The upper part adjoining benevolence gives the desire to adapt ourselves to others and to society in manners, speech, &c.

3rd. MECHANICAL COPYING.—The back part gives the sense of mechanical imitation—to take patterns of what we see.

4th. SERVILITY.—The lower part adjoining ideality gives the desire to copy others in manners, dress, fashion, speech, &c.

VERY LARGE.—Are capable of imitating to the life, can hardly speak without gesticulating; will often unconsciously mimic others, and unless self-esteem and dignity are large are likely at times to appear in the character of a buffoon; with other faculties proportionately suitable, would make an inimitable actor.

LARGE.—Have a great ability to copy and take a pattern from what you see done, are highly imitative; with good language and intuition, can mimic verbally to the life, and with good mechanical powers would excel in imitating from models, &c.

FULL.—With effort will be quite able to copy, and may succeed fairly as a mimic; yet in all that you attempt to imitate you will have to be assisted by other large faculties, or you will fail in reaching more than comparative success.

AVERAGE.—Can copy fairly, but with considerable effort may mimic some special peculiarity, but can never be versatile and clever at imitating; must trust other faculties and means for accurate copying.

MODERATE.—Can mimic little or none; with good form, size, construction, may be a good or excellent draughtsman, but are original, not imitative.

SMALL.—Are not fond of copying, dislike to do as others do, would completely fail as a mimic; decidedly inclined to originality in everything.

HEPWORTH DIXON, author and verbal delineator of character, manners, &c.—Face indicates fearlessness, unbounded self-confidence, independence, with finely-developed descriptive powers.

TOOLE, the versatile actor and man of many parts.—Face indicates a plastic and rapid comprehension of character, and ability for vigorously successful imitation.

To CULTIVATE.—As the function of this organ does not lie merely in mimicry or mechanical imitation, but in enabling us to adapt ourselves with facility to others, and to our conditions in life, its cultivation is frequently indispensable. The power to reproduce and copy preserves, not only *fac-similes* of the treasures of all ages, but enables us to partially rival nature in the reproduction of her varied types of beauty and utility. You should persist in imitating some certain desirable thing until you become master of what you attempt; should imitate everything you see worthy of imitation. Avoid singularity and exclusiveness; but try and become homogeneous with whatever society you are compelled or induced to associate with, recollecting that the perfect imitation of what we see and hear is a gift that, rightly used, may lead to fortune and fame; and if you despise the act of copying others, remember that it is only weakness to copy that which is degrading and puerile, and noble to imitate whatever is grand, beautiful, and true.

To RESTRAIN.—To do this resolutely avoid every form of plagiarism within your power; be yourself, individual and original. If you are a mechanic, artist, orator, writer, or man of business, seek to set up your own models, and accept a copy only from necessity. Don't be afraid of a little singularity of dress and manners. Choose to be independent. What your friend or neighbour does, that don't you do simply BECAUSE they did it. Dress for elegance and comfort, not for fashion, remembering that the servility of fashionable usages is a degrading toadyism, unworthy of an original or independent man or woman. Follow nature, not art or artifice, and you may eventually shake off a yoke of bondage that involuntarily compels you to do what your dignity and better judgment would condemn.

AN AZTEC.—Indicating little brain power and no reason; harmless, but idiotic; no wit or humour.

DICKENS.—A contour denoting marvellously minute and accurate perception, along with power of verbal and mimetic delineation, large humour and mirth, acute sensitiveness, with indomitable will and independence.

MIRTHFULNESS.

Sense of the absurd, ludicrous, and funny; the foundation of wit and humour. We give it four conditions :

1st. SENSE OF WIT.—The inner part adjoining causality and comparison gives the power of spontaneous witticism, the apt and witty retort or repartee.

2nd. SENSE OF HUMOUR.—The lower part gives the capacity for humour, droll sayings, and general jollity of disposition.

3rd. SENSE OF THE LUDICROUS.—The outer part gives a sense of the ludicrous and grotesque in manners, actions, such as the broad face, the pantomimic, &c.

4th. PLEASANTRY.—The upper part gives the sense of general pleasantness of feeling and speech, the jocular, bantering, &c.

VERY LARGE.—Are exceedingly quick and apt at turning everything into ridicule; are disposed to throw off constant sallies of wit; facetious to a fault; and unless you have benevolence, dignity, and good judgment to restrain you, may find yourself dreaded and disliked. With large imitation and sociability, would be popular, though perhaps feared by all.

LARGE.—Are highly disposed to be witty ; a keen sense of the ludicrous and comical; are fond of making fun for others. With large imitation, would make an excellent actor. With a good intellect, would write and speak racily and wittily; but if the organization is coarse and dignity deficient, will be very liable to indulge in witticisms that are neither creditable nor manly. Without intellectual acuteness, are more fond of fun than capable of producing it.

FULL.—Have a good share of mirthful feeling; can relish jokes highly, but are not constantly witty. With large comparison and combativeness, would be ironical or bitter; with large hope and benevolence, cheerful and genial in witticism. Can be grave and earnest; have wit and humour principally when strongly called out; or with small comparison would be less really witty than a lover of funny and grotesque things.

AVERAGE.—Can perceive jokes and relish fun, but are not gifted with wit and humour. May with the assistance of other powerful faculties exhibit occasional flashes of wit, but the character is not ruled by it; are generally grave and sober.

MODERATE.—Have now and then witty ideas only. Can appreciate fun fairly with the assistance of good comparison and perception, but will not lay out much in either time or money to gratify your risibilities.

SMALL.—Will make little or no fun, are generally stolid and straight-faced ; with large reverence and dignity, will frown on everything approaching to fun or levity ; are, toad-like, "immobile" when fun is going.

To CULTIVATE.—You should first understand that this is an intellectual faculty, the cultivation of which is equally important with that of reason. It adjoins reason or causalty, and assists the judgment in ascertaining the true or false by seeing the congruity or incongruity of ideas and suggestions. Its cultivation is also a valuable aid to health by stimulating cheerfulness, and preventing over-seriousness and despondency, assisting digestion and placidity of feeling. You should recollect that true wit is the most popular, and perhaps the highest, order of intellectuality. The gifted and original man of wit is the leader of every assembly—the master of ceremonies in public or private ; for he can annihilate whole edifices of reason and logic by a few brilliant and witty verbal flourishes. He may not be a reasoner or thinker ; not a man of science or mathematics ; but if he is truly witty he is more than equal to all. You should read the works of the principal humourists ; witness comedy, not tragedy ; learn amusing anecdotes, and excite mirth in others by relating them, bearing in mind the fact that man is the only animal that can laugh, but that he laughs because he is more than an animal.

To RESTRAIN.—This is essential when perverted wit leads into buffoonery, or when we pain and injure others by constant lampooning and ridicule. Let benevolence and dignity guide you, and under such control you need not be afraid of being witty ; especially don't allow yourself to be constantly amused with childish trifles ; be serious, earnest, manly, or womanly ; don't laugh in the wrong place ; and learn that to be merely jolly or funny will at length weary your most intimate friend ; don't make it your highest ambition to earn the sobriquet of "jolly fellow," as you can be that, and not be very high ; let your witticisms be always subordinate to good taste and a cultivated judgment; and try and realize the great fact that there is a time both for weeping and laughing, and that life is not a perpetual joke.

DARWIN.—Immensely-developed observing and classifying faculties, average reason, deficient spirituality, great will and practicality, large individuality.

CARLYLE.—Small perceptives, great reason, low hope, intense thoughtfulness and sympathy, a large brain, strong friendship, with rugged independence and vigour.

INDIVIDUALITY.

Power of physical observation; rapid identification and comprehension of natural objects or ideas; desire to see. We give it three conditions:

1st. DESIRE FOR SEEING.—The lower part gives the desire to notice and examine physical objects.

2nd. MENTAL OBSERVATION.—The upper part gives the power to quickly comprehend ideas and suggestions of an internal bearing.

3rd. INQUISITIVENESS.—The middle part gives the inquisitive and curious disposition—a desire to know from mere curiosity.

VERY LARGE.—Are insatiable in your desire to see, know, and examine everything; a rapid and definite observer, eager to know all, see all, and comprehend all, and if memory is strong enough to retain what you collect, would in time be a walking encyclopædia.

LARGE.—Have a great desire to see and know all that is passing around you; are very quick of perception; have presence of mind, and readiness in understanding whatever is told or shown to you; without a good memory, however, may be incapable of retaining a tithe of what this faculty presents to your mind.

FULL.—Are rather observing and specific in individual comprehension of objects and ideas; capable of much quickness of perception, and if memory is proportionately good would make a rather apt scholar; but with deficient reflective faculties would not sufficiently digest what is present to your mind.

AVERAGE.—Have some curiosity to see and examine, but will be occasionally slow in grasping and comprehending the nature of what you see and hear; will perhaps forget names, or lose PRESENT recollection of a circumstance, yet with a reasonable time to think and examine will show no special deficiency.

MODERATE.—Are rather deficient in palpable, ready observation; occasionally absent-minded, or recollect when too late; not sufficiently wide awake in reference to surroundings, and if reflection and continuity are large will find much difficulty in applying your mind to new objects; with these deficient, may do fairly.

SMALL.—Are quite weak in physical perception, often absent-minded, and unless sustained by other large faculties this deficiency will unfit you for many practical pursuits.

To CULTIVATE.—As this faculty affects both perceptive and reflective intellect, its cultivation in this practical age is highly important. Many great scholars have been deficient of it, but those with versatility of cleverness and great power of adapting and applying their knowledge invariably have it large. There are some pursuits in which it is indispensable (those who have to superintend others) to decide quickly—as men or women of business, barristers, doctors, and school teachers; it is rapidly cultivated by travel, by artistical pursuits and drawing, by waiting on customers in a shop, and in all pursuits in which the mind is outwardly and constantly on the alert; you should avoid all unnecessary pondering, and seek constant means of observation ; take stock of whatever meets the eye, and live more in sympathy with surrounding objects and influences.

To RESTRAIN.—This is necessary when we are led into a meddling curiosity to feed the vision with every insignificant and passing object or circumstance, to the exclusion of matters of importance ; you should remember that its excessive action renders the mind superficial, a mere objectless kaleidoscope of evanescent impressions ; when you see others gape and gaze, shut your eyes and think ; don't go with the crowd after novelty, but devote much time to reading and contemplation ; resolve to learn few things, but learn them well and digest them after learning ; walk with your head reflectively, not thrown back, and determine to be more thorough and less superficial.

FORM.

Sense and recollection of shape, configuration, outline, faces, &c. &c. We give it three conditions :

1st. MEMORY OF FACES.—The upper part adjoining individuality gives the power to recollect features and general expression.

2nd. OBJECT FORMING.—The outer part next to *size* gives the power to form objects, such as in drawing, &c.

3rd. ARTISTIC REGULARITY.—The inner and lower part gives the sense of artistic harmony in physical objects.

VERY LARGE.—Will never forget the countenance of persons and form of things once arresting attention; will (if eyesight is good) understand shapes at a great distance; with equally large size would draw to the life.

LARGE.—Will remember distinctly for a long period everything that has a definite shape; are extremely fond of harmony in forms; will know by sight numbers of persons whom you may be unable to name; with size and constructiveness large would succeed in designing and drawing, and with colour large have the leading faculties for a good artist.

FULL.—Will recognise persons' countenances, &c., with considerable accuracy, but may make occasional mistakes ; with other perceptive organs prominent would show no marked deficiency ; could probably draw fairly with attention and practice.

AVERAGE.—Have a fair recollection of external shapes and forms, but are by no means gifted in this branch of memory ; would require to keep the object before your eye to draw well; may not entirely forget, but will often only partially recollect faces, &c.

MODERATE.—Are quite liable to make mistakes in persons unless you pay especial attention to observing them; could not draw and shape objects without much difficulty, would require compass and rule.

SMALL.—Have a very indistinct recollection of persons, shapes, &c. ; liable to be constantly mistaken.

To CULTIVATE.—There is no method of cultivation equal to that of systematically *drawing* the form of every object worthy of notice. Studying the varied forms of the thousands of figures and faces we see, and trying to reproduce them by lines, curves, and angles, as in drawing; the study of botany and the natural sciences generally are excellent, for the infinite and varied forms throughout nature are defined according to class and production, so there can be no deception to the eye. Correct spelling has much to do with this faculty, remembering the length and arrangement of words not pronounced phonetically. You should not allow a day to pass without trying to draw and reproduce some object that interests you.

To RESTRAIN.—This is seldom necessary, except where irregularities of shape and form are painful to the eye and affect the nervous system. The great portrait painter, Sir Thomas Lawrence, induced disease in this faculty by habitually painting persons from memory, his powerful *form* and other faculties retaining a distinct recollection of the sitter, and by resuming his seat at his easel the form of the subject appeared **exactly** as it appeared in reality. Hallucinations are often attributable to a diseased condition of *form.*

ANIMAL NOBILITY.—A physiognomy denoting sagacity, intuitive penetration, memory, devotedness, dignity, courage, along with all the higher animal instincts; a noble dog.

HARRISON WEIR, the Artist and Animal Draughtsman.—A contour indicating large perception, power of accurate measurement, strong independence and vigour of character, without great brilliancy of imagination, large size form, &c.

SIZE.

The sense of bulk, magnitude, proportion; power to judge of relative size and weight of objects. We give it three conditions:

1st. ESTIMATING DISTANCE.—The outer part of the faculty adjoining *weight* gives the power to estimate distances, and assists weight, as in shooting, throwing, &c.

2nd. ESTIMATING PROPORTION.—The inner part next to *form* gives the power to estimate the relation which one object bears toward another—assisting form, as in drawing.

3rd. JUDGMENT OF BULK.—The middle part gives the power of readily computing bulk, as telling the weight, diameter, size, &c. of any article or object.

VERY LARGE.—Possess a wonderful accuracy in determining the size and relative bulk of objects, are intuitively correct, and will require little or no aid from measuring appliances.

LARGE.—Are a good judge of bulk, an excellent talent for measuring proportion and the relative sizes of objects; of detecting errors in supposed perpendiculars and angles; with large weight added would excel as a marksman, with large form would draw with great accuracy.

FULL.—Can measure distances and estimate bulk tolerably well, but will show no remarkable talent in it; with other faculties correspondingly large will show no palpable deficiency, but will not be equal to judging hairs'-breadths by the eye.

AVERAGE.—Can measure bulk, but not sufficiently well to dispense with measuring appliances; will find yourself occasionally mistaken in the length, breadth, and height of objects; with large form might, however, draw tolerably well.

MODERATE.—Are deficient in the talent of measuring and estimating by the eye; with practice, along with other well-developed organs, may do fairly, but must be careful about trusting your judgment.

SMALL.—Are liable to be quite inaccurate, may distinguish between mountains and molehills, but are likely to be correct only by accident, not intuition.

To CULTIVATE.—This is essential in many pursuits where weighing and estimating are required. Valuers, dealers in stock, grocers, architects and builders, engineers, &c., require it fully or largely developed. It is indispensable to the draughtsman and artist, and by aiding quantities and proportion is a valuable assistance to mathematicians and men of letters. You should study the laws of physical gradation, and try to estimate the relative power of each grade relatively to size. Freehand drawing is an excellent means of cultivation, and also the antipodean studies of astronomy and microscopical researches; its cultivation, however, will largely depend on the pursuit in which you are engaged.

To RESTRAIN is seldom necessary, except you acquire a measuring mania, and are incessantly pained by witnessing disproportion, in which case strive to learn that irregularity of size, as well as form and colour, to a great extent constitutes nature's harmony.

WEIGHT.

Balancing power, sense of gravity, power to climb, ride, preserve equilibrium and steadiness of physical action. We give it three conditions :

1st. POWER TO EQUIPOISE.—The outer portion of the faculty gives the power of physical control and steadiness, as in balancing, &c.

2nd. SENSE OF FORCE IN MACHINERY.—The inner part adjoining size gives the capacity to appreciate the resisting power in machinery and other objects in motion, to obtain mechanical equilibrium.

3rd. MENTAL STEADINESS.—The middle part gives the power of mental coolness, steadiness of hand and aim, as in shooting, throwing, &c.

VERY LARGE.—Have a wonderful power of balancing, climbing, and can determine the force of resistance and weight with astonishing accuracy; would feel at home aloft or in a balloon.

LARGE.—Could walk well on a high, narrow place, ride gracefully with practice, shoot correctly, have a cool and steady head and hand, and are hardly likely to lose your footing; would enjoy the sense of motion, dancing, &c.

FULL.—Will ordinarily keep your centre of gravity well; but with caution large, would venture little; with practice, could ride well, and balance your body easily and rather gracefully in walking, &c.; are fully able to estimate gravity and resistance.

AVERAGE.—Will balance yourself fairly, but will not be noted for riding or climbing talent—would never rival Blondin, and with large caution will be much more fond of *terra firma* than aerial suspension.

Moderate.—Have a deficient sense of balancing power, a timidity or uncertainty in climbing, and would be unsuitable for any pursuit requiring coolness at a high elevation ; are not sailor-like.

Small.—Have little or no perception of gravity, easily thrown down and lose your footing, will never succeed as a balloonist.

To **Cultivate.**—As this faculty gives steadiness, ease, and a certain gracefulness to all our physical movements, its cultivation is often very important. All first-class marksmen, equestrians, dancers, and acrobats, have it large. It is necessary to the engineer and machinist in comprehending the force and resisting power in various parts of machinery, and it is indispensable to the mathematical astronomer who weighs worlds and computes the forces of attraction and repulsion. You should as far as possible practice climbing, riding, turn acrobatic, practise sleight of hand, walk, dance, run, and endeavour to render yourself as aerial as is consistent with human methods of locomotion.

To **Restrain** is necessary when the faculty prompts you to abandon useful duties to become a mountebank. Recollect that it is a gift in which monkeys excel men under all circumstances, and a fame won by its exercise as far from being the highest of rational and noble achievements.

COLOUR.

Sense of colour in nature, perception of gradation of tints, power to match colours and perceive their distinction as in the rainbow, kaleidoscope, chromatrope, &c. We give it three conditions :

1st. **Recollection of Colour.**—The lower part of the faculty gives the sense of colour, memory, the power to recall colours once seen.

2nd. **Perspective Gradation.**—The upper part gives the sense of colour perspective, as in proper force required to produce distance, nearness, &c.

3rd. **Harmony.**—The outer part of the faculty adjoining order gives the sense of harmony and fitness of colour, as in contrast, &c.

Very Large.—Have an intense love of colour, are delighted with pictures in which great harmony of colour is displayed, a wonderful recollection of tints and colours.

Large.—Have a superior talent for arranging, comparing, and mingling colours, and with other faculties suitably developed are capable of a high degree of artistic talent, in reproducing tints, &c., that you see ; with defective form and size would colour well, but fail in drawing.

Full.—With practice would succeed very well in mingling and using colours, but without practice would not excel, yet with large form, size, &c., would be capable of achieving success in art.

Average.—Are not inclined to notice colours so closely as other matters ; with much practice would be fairly successful, but may notice a great many things without being able to recollect much about their colour.

Moderate.—If aided by great practice might be able to discern and arrange colours, so as not to appear crude or violent in contrast, but will find considerable difficulty in distinguishing colours by artificial light.

Small.—Are almost colour blind, have little or no conception of colour, and are constantly liable to make mistakes.

To **Cultivate.**—It is first necessary to appreciate the fact that it is to colour we owe nearly all the beauties that we see in nature, and that a perception of colour is a true sense of harmony. You should consequently learn that the improvement of this organ is a harmonizing, refining influence. You must simply practice your power both by daylight and artificial light in the perpetual sense of contrast and complemental tints, count the hues of the rainbow, and impress their blendings on your memory. Notice in the summer or autumn landscape the grey of distance gracefully merging into the rich and varied hues at your feet; arrange and classify the flower tints, and study carefully the result of the blending and mingling of the three primary colours, out of which nature girds herself in the panoply of a myriad hues; and if you are palpably deficient you should gain the assistance of a friend in selecting your colours as to dress, &c., so as to avoid violent contrast. In short, never neglect an opportunity in putting the faculty on the rack of observation, and you may learn to see beauties that would else have remained hidden.

To Restrain.—This is only necessary where a passion for colour has a tendency to produce disharmony by obliterating the beauty of form. You should reflect that there are other harmonies in nature that demand equal attention, and excessive attention to colour destroys harmony. Endeavour to appreciate the subdued and grey, the beauty of form and proportion, and that grace and loveliness may exist where colour holds little or no place. The colourless marble statue had a bewitching grace, which the artistically enamoured Greek worshipped as his goddess.

ORDER.

Sense of arrangement, neatness, method, and system. We give it three conditions:

1st. Neatness.—The part next to colour gives the desire for order, precision, and exactness in the relation which one thing bears to another.

2nd. System.—The outer part next to calculation gives the sense of methodical arrangement, working on a plan, &c.

3rd. Love of Detail.—A general fulness of the faculty, along with other combinations, such as ideality, &c., gives a sense of detail, minute finish, &c.

Very Large.—Are excessively precise and particular about having every little thing in its proper place; are tormented by disorder, fastidious: if ideality and nervous temperament are large, are liable to induce illness by fretting and worrying over every trifling disarrangement.

Large.—Will have everything in its proper place if possible; are very fond of system, and can find in the dark what you require; if energy is equally strong will excel in methodical arrangement; with large ideality will be scrupulously exact.

Full.—Are fond of order, and will generally keep it, but are not fastidious; if your nature is otherwise ease-loving will be orderly, as it suits your mood; but with large ideality and energy are not likely to show any lack of method and system.

Average.—Are inclined to appreciate order, yet are not sufficiently exact for a pursuit where great method and arrangement are required; if energy and artistical feelings are strong will display no special lack of order, yet with these deficient would be decidedly wanting in system for practical success.

Moderate.—May like order, but do not sufficiently keep it: if otherwise careless of property or money would allow confusion and waste; with large form, ideality, &c., would show power of artistical arrangement, but are decidedly too unsystematic.

Small.—Are nearly destitute of the feeling of order and system; likely to be always in a muddle, and unless other motives and faculties step in to assist you will have your affairs in irretrievable confusion.

To Cultivate.—We can hardly over-estimate the importance of the cultivation of this faculty. Order is said to be heaven's first law. Its

Eskimo Woman.—Indicating strong affections and kindness, but an absence of order, ideality, or refinement; a vague intellect.

The Lady.—A face indicating refinement, taste, artistical feeling, activity, and great love of order and system, with great benevolence and love of pets and children.

defective action causes the failure and ruin of thousands; for great talents are often squandered by their unsystematic mode of application. You should recollect that nothing definite and important in life can be achieved without system. Orderly habits render you punctual, and consequently true to your duties and your engagements, whether in social life or business. Everything you attempt, great or small, should be based on system, and a rigid account kept of all income and expenditure. Let nothing lag behind. Collect your accounts and pay your debts when due. Don't keep saying, "Time enough," but forestall time by doing the to-morrow's work to-day, if you can. Plan out your day's work before you begin it, and when you begin it, finish it. Don't consider that you waste time by being orderly. System and a place for everything always economises time, and leaves additional time on your hands for recreation or pleasure. Do not think anything is "well enough" when it is not as well done as it can be. Consider that everything worth doing at all is worthy of being well done; and this should be your motto—Punctuality in business, system in work, and perfection in every detail.

To Restrain.—This is necessary when you are threatening to become a miserable fidget by worrying over every little item in life's journey. You should learn as far as possible to be artistically careless, so long as there is no real confusion. Leave the chairs and tables alone; and when they are pushed a hair's-breadth from their usual angle, "let them be."

Learn to be graceful, easy, artistical, natural. Take the starch and primness out of your manners, and become flexible, and try and avoid carrying your frigid scruples into the little ins and outs of social life, as you make others uncomfortable and yourself miserable; and remember that excessive fastidiousness makes the journey of life painful and harassing.

CALCULATION.

Capacity of reckoning, estimating numbers, and numerical calculations in business estimates. We give it three conditions :

1st. RECOLLECTING FIGURES.—The part next to order gives the power of rapid calculation, and the systematical relation of figures to each other.

2nd. ESTIMATING AND VALUING.—The outer part gives the power to comprehend profit and loss in business, to understand value of articles by computation.

3rd. MATHEMATICS.—A general fulness of the organ, along with intellect, gives the mathematical talent; the solution by figures of what reason would analyse and comprehend.

VERY LARGE.—Have a remarkable talent for reckoning; can do the most complicated calculations in your head. With a large intellect would excel in the higher mathematics.

LARGE.—Are capable of grasping and understanding arithmetical calculations with great comparative ease; could become a rapid accountant; and, with good continuity, would retain columns of figures and their products consecutively and clearly.

FULL.—Are rather favourably developed in calculating powers, and with practice and a good degree of continuity would succeed, or perhaps even excel, in book-keeping, &c.; have sufficient of this power for ordinary business purposes, though not a prodigy.

AVERAGE.—With practice and rules would show favourable powers of calculating, estimating, &c.; but unless the faculty is well supported by continuity, comparison, and other faculties, would not show any remarkable talent in figures.

MODERATE.—Are rather deficient in arithmetical powers; will get confused occasionally, and forget necessary figures; will require the constant support of other faculties to enable you to manage your business.

SMALL.—Are more often incorrect than correct in dividing, subtracting, &c., easily confused and constantly liable to make mistakes, with an otherwise weak memory would be an arithmetical blunderer.

To CULTIVATE.—The improvement of this faculty is essential not only to business success but also to assist the faculty of order in maintaining method and regularity of action. He who honestly and carefully calculates seldom fails; it gives many a dull intellect success; for the chances of success or failure are all forecast by the safety of mechanical estimates. You should not only acquire the ordinary rules of arithmetic, but reckon up constantly in your head all the items of your daily transactions. Think of a certain number of figures, and mentally work out the result, making memory as far as possible "responsible." Calculate beforehand profit and loss, count the cost, and turn yourself as far as possible into a calculating-machine, so that while you may not rival "Babbages" you may avoid awkward and serious blunders.

To RESTRAIN.—This is only necessary where figures become a mania. In a lunatic asylum in Canada was a lunatic whose disease was "arithmetic," and every moment of his waking hours was devoted to filling large folios with the most absurd calculations. A certain New England Yankee became one of the greatest bores in the community by his mania of estimating the results of every business enterprise projected or alluded to by his friends and neighbours.   He earned the sobriquet of the *Walking Decimal.*   You should use figures only when compelled to, and relieve your mind instantly by turning to something else of greater importance.   Remember that life is not merely a sum in arithmetic or an algebraic problem.

RUSKIN, the Art Critic.—Great perception, locality, comparison, and power of discrimination; a platonic nature, leading to fastidiousness.

FROUDE, the Historian.—Deficient perception physically; a high brain, intellectually critical, brilliant but not great powers.

LOCALITY.

Memory of places, geographical talent, ability to locate what has been once seen, desire to travel.   We give it four conditions :

1st. EXPLORING.—The lower part of the organ gives the desire for new explorations, to visit distant lands.

2nd. GEOGRAPHICAL MEMORY.—The inner part next individuality gives the power to recall to the mind places once visited.

3rd. LOCAL MINUTENESS.—The upper part next eventuality gives the power of local exactness, as in finding a page or putting the hand on an article in the dark, &c.

4th. LOVE OF TRAVEL.—A general fulness of the organ, along with other faculties, activity, &c., gives a restlessness, a desire to wander about irrespective of place.

VERY LARGE.—Have an excessive love of travelling and exploring; would see the world if you could, and have a distinct and vivid memory of places once visited; with small continuity and inhabitiveness would be always on the move.

LARGE.—Have an excellent recollection of places, will seldom lose yourself even in the dark; would enjoy travel exceedingly; with large friendship and inhabitiveness might not travel, but would learn geography with facility, and recollect the *locale* of every place or thing once seen.

FULL.—Will recollect places well, yet are liable to occasionally lose yourself in

E

difficult roads or streets; but with other large perceptive organs need seldom be liable to do so.

AVERAGE.—Have a fair memory of places, &c., once visited, but will be likely to recollect other matters and incidents better; with large comparison would recollect places very well by associative circumstances.

MODERATE.—Will recollect places rather poorly; liable to get lost unless you pay strict attention to objects by the way; with an otherwise observing nature, however, you may not experience great difficulty; would not be a Livingstone or a Columbus in geographical talent.

SMALL.—Are decidedly weak in local memory, easily confused, lose your way and place, and are constantly liable to be in a maze.

To CULTIVATE.—The improvement of this talent is valuable, not only to give readiness and directness of local knowledge, but to assist other phases of memory, by supplying links of associative recollection; it assists historical memory, by recalling the mind to geographical position where events happened, as it fixes every *locale* or spot accurately in the mind. You should, if possible, travel, and while travelling promote the wide-awake feeling; and in retracing your ground, learn to identify the position of each place, preserving a mental map in memory. If you cannot travel, study landscape pictures, geography, draw maps, read books of travel, especially those illustrated, such as Cassell's, &c. Avoid hugging the fireside corner, but go wherever you can find objects of interest, as by so doing you will not only improve local memory, but you may store your mind with priceless knowledge.

To RESTRAIN.—Don't convert yourself into a perambulating-machine, but rest satisfied with the little world around you. Don't ever wander vaguely; better study one grand picture than a thousand poor ones. Avoid reading tempting books of travel; they only make you restless. Leave excursions to the invalids and jaded denizens of the city, and resolutely turn your mind into some other absorbing channel, recollecting that the world is too wide for you to see it all, and you had better accumulate sources of happiness at home. Remember the adage of the rolling stone.

EVENTUALITY.

Recollection of events, historical power, power to treasure up facts, circumstances, &c. We give it three conditions:

1st. HISTORY.—The upper part, joining comparison, gives the historical power, with good continuity, to trace events in connection with each other.

2nd. PASSING EVENTS.—The lower part, next to individuality, gives the power to collect and relate passing occurrences, without any special association.

3rd. ASSOCIATIVE MEMORY.—The middle part gives the power to retain the connection of passing or past events, as they associate themselves with personal or national history.

VERY LARGE.—Will never fully forget any occurrence, have an astonishing memory, and a craving desire to accumulate hoards of facts, statistics, incidents, &c.; with large continuity, are inclined to dwell upon the minutest details.

LARGE.—Have a clear and retentive memory of general news, historical facts, anecdotes, &c.; and with equal intellectual power in other faculties, and continuity, would enjoy a really first-class historical memory.

FULL.—Will recollect leading events and important facts, but will occasionally forget details; without good associative powers, would frequently do so; but if continuity and comparison are large, will experience little difficulty in recalling anything you want.

AVERAGE.—Have only a fair recollection; will now and then feel disappointed, from inability to recall events, &c., that you require; with assisting faculties, such as continuity, &c., fully developed, may not exhibit any apparent deficiency to others, though are likely to feel it yourself.

MODERATE.—Have not a good memory of occurrences; can recall generalities, but will frequently lose details; with defective continuity, will find your recollection very disconnected and uncertain.

SMALL.—Have a treacherous and often confused memory of events; and it is only by the assistance of other large faculties that your memory in this particular will not be allowed to fall into irretrievable confusion; with small continuity, will be in a constant medley from a treacherous recollection.

SHAKESPEARE, the Poet of all time.—A splendid balance of brain, with great memory, and high organic quality.

INDIAN, of Brazil.—A degraded physiognomy, showing a lack of memory and intellectual refinement.

To CULTIVATE.—The cultivation of this faculty is of the very highest importance; for, standing in the centre of the intellectual group, it seems to be a mentor, or a central office from which other parts of the intellect draw their supplies. It may to a great extent be called the storehouse of the intellect. Without this faculty and that of *time* we should have no history or chronology, and the rapidity with which events occur in this transition age has a tendency rather to weaken its action, as there is seldom time for the events to impress themselves on the mind. You should habitually read history, and digest well what you read; review the events of each day at its close; commit to memory interesting anecdotes and circumstances, and acquire the habit of relating them; keep a diary or journal, and don't allow any one of the three hundred and sixty-five days in the calendar to pass without having recorded some fact worth remembering, and by so doing, no matter how indifferent your memory may be, you will discover that systematic cultivation will cause even a feeble organ to do wonders.

To RESTRAIN.—This is rarely necessary, unless you have such a *penchant* for story-telling that you bore everybody and are likely to be suspected of invention. Too good a memory demands a circumspect life, especially if the conscience is tender and sensitiveness great; but if there is a morbid tendency to recall insignificant facts and circumstances, set to work at once and create another and healthier channel of action.

TIME.

Recollection of dates, chronological memory, sense of the lapse of time, and keeping time in marching, in music, &c. We give it three conditions:

1st. CHRONOLOGY.—The inner part near to eventuality gives the power to recollect the lapse of time, the power of chronological recollection.

2nd. TIME IN MUSIC.—The outer part adjoining tune gives the power to beat time accurately, to keep step in walking, and to measure the pauses in melody.

3rd. PUNCTUALITY.—The lower part next to order gives the sense of punctuality in business and other engagements.

VERY LARGE.—Can remember the time of occurrences with wonderful exactness; with large eventuality would excel as a chronologist, and with large tune would be a first-class musician.

LARGE.—Have an excellent recollection of chronological incidents; can keep step, and measure the lapse of time with accuracy; are fond of perfect measure in music, &c.; highly punctual.

FULL.—Will generally appreciate the lapse of time correctly, but are not distinguished; with other associative organs large would show no deficiency; would keep step, &c., well; fond of punctuality.

AVERAGE.—Will notice dates and retain them fairly if other faculties press them upon your attention, but not without; with effort only can keep good time in music.

MODERATE.—Have a deficient sense of the lapse of time; a poor idea of dates; with large tune would succeed in music, but would find a difficulty in keeping the measure; are rather irregular in action; not punctual.

SMALL.—Have a weak chronological sense; seldom think of correct dates; find it very difficult or impossible to keep step or beat time to music; are jerky and irregular in action.

To CULTIVATE.—As a proper development of this faculty gives punctuality and evenness to our movements, its value can hardly be overestimated; without it we are fitful in action, frequently behind, and if excitable, beforehand when we should NOT be, it estimates the importance of saving time, and lays out in advance the relative periods required for the accomplishment of each object. You should never let time get ahead of you; keep a good timepiece, and make all your calculations by it— resolve to be ten minutes ahead rather than one minute late; make chronology associated with history a special study; have a good pocket-calendar to correct you when in error, at the same time charge your memory with a sense of time's value, recollecting that "time is more than money"—it is a part of life, and every fleeting moment should be usefully employed, so that none of this valuable commodity may be misspent.

To RESTRAIN is seldom necessary; but when you are worried by an excessive sense of punctuality, don't convert yourself into a chronological index; value the moments and hours of ease and relaxation as indispensable; let time glide on smoothly without incessantly noting its lapse, 'twill go on the same—calm and unruffled—after you are dead and gone.

GRISI, artiste —An harmonious face, indicating great musical and artistical capacities.

MRS. SOMERVILLE, the scientific and mathematical woman.—Earnest, thoughtful, deficient in musical ability; a face indicating positive character and will.

TUNE.

Sense of melody, modulation of sounds in speaking, power to understand and appreciate harmony. In phrenological definitions it is not always safe to mark the relative size of this faculty; its situation in reference to the angles of the brain is unfavourable to a correct estimate of its size, though it is certain that the place given to it on the phrenological map—beside its necessary coadjutor, time—is correct; yet many serious mistakes have been made in estimating it. There is perhaps no other faculty or organ that incites so much solicitous inquiry as to development as this. There is more or less of the sense of melody in every nature; but when we consider the few who achieve great success in either vocal or instrumental melody, we must consider that the love of music as yet is more a love of it than talent to produce it. It requires a great brain to make a truly great artist, and time and tune alone do not constitute the power to be a musician; they only give correct measure and "appreciation of music." To excel in producing the melody which the world admires, it requires in addition a high order of imagination, feeling, poetic sentiment, tenderness, spirituality and sympathy. There is much that is called music quite undeserving of the name, and sensitive individuals are disposed to take offence if the sound they emit—correct in measure and mathematically accurate in the octave pitch—is not dignified with the title of *melody*, even though the soul be wanting. When the faculty is marked, it is done in deference to the individual, not as a certainty. We, however, give it three conditions, which will assist the judgment in determining the extent of the musical ability.

1st. LOVE OF MUSIC.— The upper part gives the love of hearing melody and fondness for music without the direct ability of producing it.

2nd. POWER OF HARMONY.—Tho lower part gives the power to modulate the voice, as in singing and pronunciation.

3rd. MEMORY OF SOUNDS.—The inner part next *time* gives the power to retain sounds in memory, the lapse and force of sound as in recollection of voices, &c.

VERY LARGE.—Are enchanted with melody, and possess an extraordinary memory of tunes, airs, &c., once heard; with an otherwise suitable development would be a musical genius, an intense lover and producer of sweet sounds.

LARGE.—Will easily catch tunes and melodies, very fond of hearing music, have the soul and feeling of a musician, and with a large time and a favourable temperament would realize great success in it.

FULL.—Are a lover of melody, and could catch tunes by ear tolerably well, but would need help from notes; are not an intuitive genius, yet with practice may achieve a good success, but require a highly favourable development otherwise to excel.

AVERAGE.—Are rather fond of music, and if aided by notes and practice, along with an imaginative and emotional nature, would be fairly successful, but would sing and play music best when in concert with and aided by others.

MODERATE.—Are rather mechanical in musical conception, would sing and play only with great practice, and could then realize very ordinary success: if time is large and temperament sympathetic, may perform very fairly in concert, but not well alone.

SMALL.—Are nearly an automaton in melody, are not stirred or melted by it, could succeed better with a hand-organ than a violin or piano; very little conception of or soul for music.

To CULTIVATE.—As this is perhaps the most bewitching of all accomplishments, and one of the most refining, so its cultivation is highly important. It should be an important part of the early education of every child who is more or less gifted with musical ability. It can hardly be taught too young, and in that respect differs from many other branches of education. It is often the harmonizer, the good and soothing angel of tho household, and it can be at all times introduced as a relief to other and severer studies; to cultivate it, you should not aim at mechanical accuracy alone, for melody is not in mere sound, however perfect the modulation and measure. It is the soul behind that makes melody. An unfeeling but otherwise skilful player executes brilliantly on the keys of a piano. There's astonishing and wonderful accuracy, but the soul is wanting; there's a performance, but no melody; and this constitutes a large part of what is called fashionable music. Don't try to be musical because it is fashionable. Society can tolerate a "no performer" better than a bad one; but in cultivating music, simply practice, study, and closely copy the best musicians, and catch as much of their inspiration as you can. Throw your feelings into whatever you do. Don't aim at loudness, but subdued gentleness, recollecting that the soft and suppressed strains of an Æolian harp are a thousand times more pleasant to the ear than the overpowering shriek of a steam-whistle.

To RESTRAIN.—Don't turn life into a song. Make music a dessert, not a constant feast. Ascertain if your music mania is acceptable to other ears as well as your own, and resolutely shut down the safety-valve, recollecting that too much of a good thing becomes an intolerable nuisance; for even Paganini would have bored his hearers with his matchless performances on one string of a violin, if they had had Paganini always.

MARK LEMON, late Editor of *Punch*, the humorist and man of the world.—A physiognomy denoting a love of sensuous gratification, along with humour, honesty, kindness, and perceptive memory, but too little self-denial in appetite for the exhibition of the highest mental achievements.

A WESTERN INDIAN.—A face denoting the absence of wit and humour, small benevolence and imagination, great secretiveness, along with coarseness and strong animal instincts; *small language.*

LANGUAGE.

The use of words, ability to talk of what we know, verbal expressiveness, and the foundation of the lingual talent. We give it three conditions:

1st. VERBAL MEMORY.—The inner part next form gives the ability to commit to memory, to repeat verbatim what we hear or read.

2nd. VERBAL EXPRESSION.—The back and upper part as resting on the superorbital plate, and pressing the eye outward and downward, gives fluency of speech; power of expressing thoughts without committing to memory.

3rd. LINGUAL TALENT.—A general fulness of the faculty, along with large comparison and general perception, gives the power to learn languages, to be linguistically accurate in method and pronunciation.

VERY LARGE.—Are endowed with a wonderful command of words, excessively copious and redundant; unless secretiveness is large will be an incessant talker, liable to have too many words for your thoughts, and become tiresome.

LARGE.—Have great fluency and readiness of speech; seldom hesitate for words to express all that you mean. With an excitable temperament would talk with great rapidity; with intellectual and other necessary faculties proportionately strong, would excel in oratory and declamation.

FULL.—Have language enough to express yourself clearly and fully on most subjects familiar to you, but will occasionally hesitate for the right word. With a reserved nature will talk well only when aroused; with a proportionately good memory would succeed very well in relating what you know, in public speaking, &c.

AVERAGE.—Have fair ability to communicate your ideas by words, but are likely to be more select and impressive than very fluent. Will generally use familiar language, yet, with good ideality and memory along with mental vigour, could talk to good advantage when aroused; with good practice may not often hesitate.

MODERATE.—Will frequently hesitate for words; are apt to appear barren and defective in verbal expression; yet with comparison and memory large may become a good linguist, but can probably write much better than talk; are not a natural talker, apt to often repeat, &c.

SMALL.—Are certain to find a great difficulty in speaking, slow in acquiring words; may think well and write clearly, but have very little talking ability; with large secretiveness are not likely to babble anything you know.

To CULTIVATE.—Circumstances and associations have largely to do with the improvement of this organ; committing facts, ideas, anecdotes, &c., to memory, and then using the vehicle of words to relate what we have acquired at every favourable opportunity. It must be remembered that language is only a medium of expressing what other faculties remember; so that a well-stored brain is much more likely to use words with good effect. It is not wise to attempt the cultivation of language without at the same time improving general memory. There are numberless bores in society—gabblers, who are largely endowed with this faculty, but who are semi-idiotic in ideas and originality of mind. You should read much, commit to memory, carefully arrange your thoughts, and then talk, and talk to a purpose. Mingle with good talkers, and strive to catch the verbal infection. Give your thoughts wings, and if you have to wait for a word " wait." There is no practice to equal that of debating; but talk, and talk out boldly, as this faculty is susceptible of a large degree of improvement when influences are at all favourable. Don't shrug your shoulders and make helpless grimaces when you ought to speak; but speak and make your tongue responsible for imparting interest and conviction to others.

To RESTRAIN.—Remember the babbling brook, how monotonously it babbles away for ever, and think of how much more respect and awe we gaze upon a deep and silent river. Recollect that an idiot may be a clever babbler. It was said by a celebrated wit that the celebrated talker, Brougham, was much improved on his return from a foreign mission; for he had occasional flashes of silence. You should impress yourself with the fact that one anecdote well told, one fact briefly and vigorously enforced, one sentence brilliantly expressed, will give you more prestige and respect than hours of consecutive babbling. Remember the tree with myriads of leaves, but no fruit. Think of Talleyrand, the most clever and successful diplomatist of his age, with the fewest words. Reflect on the great fact that it is *knowing what to say*, and having the power to refrain from saying it, that often gives weight and confidence. Don't inflict your rhetoric on others unless you are previously certain that you can entertain and benefit them, recollecting that truest of adages, that brevity is the soul of wit.

CAUSALITY.

Intuitive knowledge of principles and causes; the reason why, comprehending laws which govern phenomena; the leading metaphysical faculty. We give it three conditions:

1st. MENTAL SUGGESTIVENESS.—The inner part adjoining comparison gives the desire for logical comprehension and explanation of principles.

2nd. CAUSE AND EFFECT.—The middle part gives the power to understand primary causes abstractedly, or apart from analogy.

3rd. DESIRE TO KNOW.—The outer part adjoining wit gives inquisitiveness and suggestiveness, the love of knowing, apart from analogical reasoning or application, originality.

VERY LARGE.—Are endowed with a great love of abstract and original ideas, an intense desire to know why; excessively abstract and thoughtful, and without a good degree of comparison are often inapt, unpractical, and misunderstood; liable to too much depth for a practical age.

LARGE.—Have a great desire to know the causes which lead to certain results, are very fond of abstract thought and reasoning, and with other intellectual faculties large, would excel in metaphysics and originality of thought; with deficient perceptive power and comparison are liable to appear vague, not enough to the point.

FULL.—Have a good degree of the original power of reason, the capability of applying means to ends, causes to effects; are likely to be more practical however than abstract; would not excel as a metaphysician, but with large comparison and memory may be a versatile and rather brilliant reasoner, if not a very deep one.

AVERAGE.—Have a fair share of the abstract quality of reason, but not profound or deep; with full or large perception would only reason from outward circumstances or events, may be highly practical, a close observer, &c.; but your intellectual powers will be manifested in another direction than that of originality of causation.

MODERATE.—Are rather deficient of the reasoning power, cannot well comprehend causes, though with large comparison and perception may show much force and point; but your mind is rather apt to rest on the surface of things, and require other parts of intellect strong to achieve success; are not long-headed.

SMALL.—Have little or no idea of cause and effect, can seldom give a reason why, and unless well endowed with other intellectual powers prominent will be liable to serious blunders.

SPURGEON, the Pulpit Orator.—Physiognomy indicates great mental readiness, language, practicality, memory, self-reliance, honesty, frankness, general shrewdness, and knowledge of character, without much reasoning power.

PROFESSOR HUXLEY.—A face indicating great solidity of judgment, independence, will, reasoning talent, and power of investigation, along with an absence of credulity and spirituality.

To CULTIVATE.—As many mistaken ideas have existed in connection with this faculty it is well to understand what are its real claims in connection with intellect. It has been called by some modern phrenologists the faculty which gives a "first-rate judgment and a gigantic intellect." This is evidently a mistake, as it holds only the same relative position in regard to intellectual power as any other mental faculty. Many have it large whose judgment and intellectual powers are decidedly defective both in reasoning and clear comprehension. Like every other faculty of the brain, it is only a primary instinct that prompts to investigation and ASSISTS judgment, for a gigantic intellect only springs from universal greatness. Of all the faculties in the front brain it gives the reason only, and other faculties apply what it discovers, and the very broad and comprehensive function ascribed to it has arisen from a want of appreciation of the law of mental harmony. On its cultivation depends success in many undertakings. In the brain of Newton it suggested the theory of gravitation, and many great discoverers in the sciences, mechanics, and the arts, owe the source of their knowledge to the *diving down* and exploring power of this organ. It suggests a cause for all phenomena; never rests satisfied with the acceptance of a truth, however palpable to the other senses, until the origin and force of that truth is fully understood. Scientific study of all kinds, especially those of an abstract nature rather than of classification, is necessary; chemistry and geology, astronomy and mathematics, the laws and principles which regulate human actions, as in history, musing, and contemplation; it is usually active in the heads of children of dawning intelligence, and grows less as other faculties have learned sufficient to set the wondering and querying mind at rest.

To RESTRAIN.—To do this be practical and wide awake, interest and busy yourself about that which is known and understood, and let the inner "hidden world" alone. Especially avoid prolixity, as too much abstract reason is not suited to this matter-of-fact and restless age. Cease learning in a new field, but apply well what you do know. Remember that thoughtful individuals are not often popular, and are often unsuccessful, as too many (*reasons*) are distasteful, and too deep thinking unfits the mind for the practical duties of life. To depress the action of this faculty, other faculties, especially the perceptive powers, should be well employed, and classification rather than discovery attended to.

COMPARISON.

The power of contrasting and comparing, analogical and inferential reasoning, criticising, and studying effects. We give it three conditions:

1st. COMPARING IDEAS.—The outer part, next to causality, gives the power of analogical reasoning, the symbolical and illustrative talent.

2nd. PHYSICAL CONTRAST.—The lower part gives the sense of contrast between physical objects, distinctions of general form and quality.

3rd. CRITICISM.—The upper part, adjoining intuitiveness, gives the disposition to criticise, pick flaws, and make mental distinctions.

VERY LARGE.—Are endowed with an extraordinary power of rapid criticism, see faults and inconsistencies at a glance, excessively disposed to analyze, and with a good memory would illustrate your ideas with wonderful clearness.

LARGE.—Have a ready and happy talent for comparing and criticising. for classifying, drawing inferences, and of understanding what is or is not analogous; with good language, could learn languages quickly; with large perception, could excel in the natural sciences.

FULL.—Will be able to illustrate and analyse well, especially if aided by good powers of physical perception; can see striking analogies and differences readily, are rather fond of drawing deductions, but for good success the faculty must be well aided.

AVERAGE.—May perceive striking analogies; but if the temperament is rather heavy and dull, will often fail in quick mental perception; with large physical perception and not large causality, may show much aptness in drawing a conclusion, but are not intuitively critical or sharp.

MODERATE.—Are rather defective in analogical power, not critical or mentally sharp in ready illustration, want time to think, and unless well supported by other parts of intellect will often seem dull to comprehend.

SMALL.—Are nearly destitute of this power, will fail in seeing differences, and a similarity or distinction must be very broad and striking to give you any conception of it; if perceptive organs are weak will be exceedingly inapt, a slow-coach.

To CULTIVATE.—This being one of the principal reasoning faculties its cultivation is highly important; it materially assists wit by giving the distinction between the grotesque and natural, as many who have this faculty large and active pass in society for being witty by their rapid and vigorous powers of repartee and illustration. As the primary sense of wit would frequently be lost for want of an analogy, it is fully developed in the heads of all clever critics and humorists, though many have it large who are not witty. You should study those subjects which demand careful analysis—chemistry, botany, mineralogy, &c., and exercise your critical and debating powers whenever available; learn to value symbols, figures of speech, and illustrative methods while talking; constantly compare, mentally and physically; and while learning that no two things in the world are exactly alike, you will also learn that two individuals believing the same ideas and truths may perversely quibble over hairs'-breadths of argumentative distinctions.

To RESTRAIN.—As it is the essential function of this faculty to criticise —and cynically-critical individuals are generally hated and dreaded—so you must learn how far your feeling tends toward adverse and deprecating criticisms either of the persons or opinions of others; especially avoid picking flaws and defects, as it is not yet time for the world to be perfect, and instead of criticising imperfections learn to value them as complemental and a "set-off" to the perfections that you DO recognise; don't keep saying "that reminds me," or, "that is just like," but study causes more and results less, remembering that the most successful critics are those whose intellectual powers are harmoniously developed, and not strained in one direction.

INTUITION, OR JUDGMENT OF CHARACTER.

Power of detecting and understanding motives and actions, perception of character, sagacious discrimination. We give it three conditions :

1st. READING CHARACTER.—The lower part next to comparison gives the power to study character by discerning the contrasts chiefly in a physiognomical sense.

2nd. PERCEPTION OF MOTIVES.—The upper part gives the power to see the internal springs which guide actions; a sense of intuitive foresight; prophetical.

3rd. SUSPICION.—The middle part or perhaps a general fulness of the faculty, along with large perception and but moderate friendship, gives the sense of suspicion, watchfulness, &c.

VERY LARGE.—You are remarkable for intuitional power of reading motives, are constantly criticising others, and unless you have good benevolence and sympathy are apt to be suspicious constantly, perhaps of your best friends.

LARGE.—You have a good faculty of rapidly judging character, are seldom deceived, will often decide about others without exactly knowing why; with large perceptive organs would read character with great clearness.

FULL.—You can generally tell on a first appearance whether you would like or dislike persons, and are not often disappointed; with large observing organs could mostly trust your first impressions, yet unless well sustained by other faculties will occasionally find yourself mistaken; with good benevolence will not be usually suspicious.

AVERAGE.—Can judge striking differences in character, and may take some pleasure in studying them, but are liable to be occasionally deceived; must study actions as well as faces to be successful; with large perceptive faculties and comparison may show good discrimination.

MODERATE.—Are liable to be frequently deceived in the character of those whom you meet; should be careful about depending on first or hasty impressions; may be able with large perception to realize striking points, but are not at all gifted with intuitional discernment.

SMALL.—Are an indifferent judge of persons; more often wrong than when you judge hastily; are not suspicious enough, and are too apt to treat all alike according to your other feelings.

To CULTIVATE.—As there are many thousands of dupes and knaves in society, so the proper cultivation of this organ would guard the one and guard against the other. A certain amount of suspicion is indispensable to safety in all pursuits where "trust" has to be reposed in others, or in social life where friendship and the proprieties have to be observed. This is an indispensable power, and it enables individuals to obey St. Paul's injunction, "Being all things TO all," for it comprehends the differences in each, and along with benevolence and judgment would suggest the method of adaptation to each. The study of human nature is indispensable to its cultivation, as it appeals directly to the source and direction of human actions, detects imposition, and understands the source and value of actions. You should not trust others till you *prove* them worthy of trust; and in all matters of business or friendly confidences, learn that politeness and wariness should go hand in hand; all good works treating on physiognomy and character, all writings that deal with matters of subtle analysis, should be studied. In short, be a detective, and while preserving the appearance of confidence, by uniformity of courtesy and kindness, never give the key of either your heart or pocket into the keeping of a stranger.

To RESTRAIN.—To do this it is necessary to first learn that suspicion and jealousy are among the most hateful of human feelings. You must learn that there are but few but who can be reached and influenced by judicious trust and kindness, but that suspicion repels all, and is destructively alienating to every phase of human love and friendship. Don't be afraid to trust your friends, as, if they disappoint you, you will have a better basis of future conduct toward them; and above all do not allow the want of truth in the few embitter you against the many, as the fault may unconsciously lie in yourself. Study yourself more and others less, and encourage benevolence in every little action of life. Consider that if you think it necessary to be as wise as a serpent, you must also be as harmless as the dove; be more childlike and confiding; shut your eyes to imperfections, or try if you cannot discover more good qualities than bad ones in those whom you know. Don't be ready to suspect; accept nothing against others on doubtful hearsay; leave slander to the gossips; prying to the eaves-droppers; suspicion to the detectives; and learn that charity and faith are the most sublime of human virtues.

Sir C. Dilke, the independent and rigid Republican.—Face shows a great sense of justice, rigid opinions, dignity, deficient courtesy or general agreeableness, a rigid character.

Charles Mattiews, the young "old" actor.—A face expressing unbounded cheerfulness, agreeableness, ease of manners, wit, and youthfulness; a plastic character.

AGREEABLENESS.

The desire to please and interest others, suavity of manner, politeness, and blandness of demeanour. We can hardly regard this as a fully ascertained faculty, as the power to be agreeable and pleasant may easily be supposed to exist in a combination of other faculties, such as sociability, approbation, benevolence, mirth, imitation, &c. It MAY exist as a separate faculty where its professed discoverer has placed it, but its existence is at least problematical. It is, however, here given as a faculty for convenience in defining character. We give it three conditions:

1st. Ease of Manners.—The power of being and feeling at ease under all circumstances, irrespective of formal courtesy or politeness.

2nd. Blandness.—The power to be conciliating and smooth in speech, to use polite and agreeable phrases.

3rd. Adaptation.—The power and desire to be pliable and mould ourselves to others and to circumstances, to fall into the current.

Very Large.—Are remarkable for the desire and capacity to render yourself agreeable and pleasant to others, to be all things to all men; cannot bear to say or do an offensive thing; excessively courteous; unless with good honesty and independence, are likely to be or appear insincere.

Large.—You have a natural tact in pleasing and of making yourself agreeable to whatever company you are in; with large approbation would be highly courteous and polite; will seldom, perhaps never, make enemies unless temper happens to be very excitable.

Full.—Are generally rather easy in your manners, though not remarkably so; can usually adapt yourself with good success to your surroundings; with large benevolence and approbativeness are not likely to have many enemies; with large friendship would show sufficient of this power to win friends by your courtesy.

AVERAGE.—Can be rather pleasing, but are likely to be so more according to your moods; with an excitable or passionate temper would forget to be courteous; but if temper is otherwise smooth, along with good benevolence, are not likely to over appear insincere or over affable.

MODERATE.—You are not *uniformly* agreeable, and perhaps are not sufficiently disposed to adapt yourself to the feelings and wishes of others; with a good temper may not give offence, but yet may show too much bluntness of speech; your courtesy is likely to come from benevolence or friendship, not from any love of pleasing or being polite.

SMALL.—Are decidedly deficient in general courtesy; apt to constantly say and do that which refined society would condemn; with deficient benevolence and approbation would often be uncouth and disagreeable; if you have much temper you are certain to make enemies; with large benevolence would be kind, but not courteous.

To CULTIVATE.—The improvement of this faculty is indispensable to all who are thrown into the current of business or social life. The art of pleasing is frequently the power of persuading, and it is only transcendent skill and genius that can in any walk in life dispense with it. There is no need of flattery or insincerity, as straightforwardness can always be exercised, even with the necessary compliments and courtesies of life. Don't regard it as a weakness to conform to polite usages, but rather regard them as refining and productive of good; recollect that "a soft answer turneth away wrath;" if others are rude, meet their rudeness by superior and courteous dignity, and learn that in human society the quiet force of self-possessed refinement always conquers brute force; study boors, not to imitate them, but to shun their boorishness; exercise benevolence in every action and word; avoid all disagreeable and disparaging remarks; don't be ashamed to return the salute of the beggar in the street, but strive in every way to prove that your equanimity is superior to every conflicting circumstance; in short, that you can at all times not only command your temper, but turn your enemies into trusty friends.

To RESTRAIN.—This is necessary when its excess leads to affectation and insincerity, and paying compliments for the sake of pleasing. Do not be afraid to speak the truth, and don't flatter your friends to spoil them; only be polite so far as it comports with self-respect and dignity, remembering that affectation and hypocrisy are twin sisters, and are the outgrowth of too much of this feeling overruling conscience and good judgment; learn the fact that your friends or the world will a thousand times more respect your honest and intelligent criticism, than your fulsome and undeserved praise.

MARRIAGE.

This table is only intended for those approximating to or at a marriageable age, and is intended to point out a few of the leading qualifications suitable to or indispensable in a partner for those for whom the chart of character is marked. A faithful and complete description of both parties is undoubtedly the safest mode, but where this is not available this table may be of considerable value, in directing those who feel uncertain as to the most suitable organization to correspond to their own.

As it does not properly come under the head of a chart of character, but is only supplementary to it, an additional fee of from 2s. to 3s. is always made for marking it. A dash under one or more words in each line indicates the conditions necessary.

Temperament should be	Nervous	Fibrous	Osseous	Sanguine	Lymphatic
Organic quality may or should be......	very high	superior	fair	moderate	rather low
General strength of constitution may or should be	excellent	good	fair	moderate	defective
Energy of character may or should be	great	rather high	good	moderate	deficient
General strength of mind and will should be	very great	rather high	fair	moderate	rather deficient
Calmness and self-control may or should be	very great	rather good	average	only moderate	defective
Perceptive faculties should be	very large	large	full	average	moderate
Reasoning and reflective organs should be	very large	large	full	average	moderate
Moral and religious qualities may or should be	very large	large	full	average	moderate
Cheerfulness of disposition may or should be	very great	rather good	medium	moderate	defective
Social and domestic faculties may or should be	very large	large	full	average	moderate
Self-confidence may or should be	very great	rather full	medium	only moderate	defective
Economy and general carefulness may or should be	very great	rather full	medium	moderate	defective
Order, system, and taste may or should be.............	very great	rather large	medium	moderate	defective
General agreeableness may or should be	very great	rather good	medium	moderate	defective
Colour of hair, eyes, and complexion may or should be..	very dark	rather dark	medium	rather light	very light
Plumpness or roundness may or should be	very full	rather plump	average	rather thin	thin and lean
Features may or should be ..	very round	oval	rather long	rather sharp	thin and marked

SPECIAL NOTICE.

All Letters and Communications may be addressed to

MR. HAGARTY,

At 52, Raglan Street,

Radnor Street, Hulme,

MANCHESTER.

Post Office Orders for the Magnetic Appliances should be made payable at the POST OFFICE, MOSS SIDE, MANCHESTER.

REVISED AND REDUCED PRICE LIST.

Superior Lung Invigorators, 21/-, 25/-.	Special Power, 30/-, 35/-.
Do. do. for Children, 15/-, 20/-.	do. 25/-.
Chest and Throat Protectors, 7/6, 10/6.	do. 12/6, 15/-.
Gentlemen's Stomach Belt for Indigestion, Biliousness, &c., 15/-, 21/-, 25/-.	do. 30/-, 35/-.
Ladies' Abdominal and Stomach Belts, 15/-, 21/-, 25/-.	do. 30/-, 35/-.
Spine Bands, 7/6, 10/6, 15/-.	do. 20/-, 25/-.
Sciatic Appliances, 21/-, 25/-.	do. 30/-, 35/-.
Knee Caps, 7/6, 10/6.	do. 12/6, 15/-.
Arm and Leg Appliances, for Rheumatism, &c., 7/6, 10/6.	do. 12/6, 15/-, 21/-.
Anklets, per pair, 7/6, 10/6.	do. 12/6, 15/-.
Wristlets, „ 5/6, 7/6.	do. 10/6, 12/6.
Head Caps, 21/-.	do. 25/-, 30/-.
Magnetic Soles, for Cold feet, per pair, 5/-.	do. 7/6, 10/6.

In ordering Belts it is necessary to send measurement around the waist.

All the above Articles are highly magnetic, those marked Special Power contain more Magnetism, and are most suitable for Chronic and long-standing cases; the lower priced ones are sufficient in ordinary cases. ALL are strongly made, will last for years without losing their Magnetism, can be left off or put on at pleasure without danger, and are equally effectual worn OVER the under clothing. Any of the Articles will be sent *free by post*, on receipt of a remittance to the above address.

Worn OVER the Under Clothing, NOT next the Body.

BATHS AND BATHING.

THIS is an important aid to health when properly administered, but injudicious bathing injures thousands; the strength of the system, state of the circulation, length of time in bathing, and form of bath, should all be carefully considered. The ends to be chiefly gained in bathing are a clean skin and an equal circulation; the form of bath most suitable is indicated in the list by a dash, thus |

Ordinary Warm Bath (at Evening) ....   per week.

Sponge or Towel Bath, cool (at Morning)   „

Ditto   ditto   (at Night) warm...   „

Vapour Bath (generally at Evening) ......   „

Turkish Bath   ditto   ......   „

Hip or Sitz Bath, warm ....   „

Ditto   ditto   cold ....   „

Wet Sheet Pack (Hydropathic) ....   „

Galvanic or Electric Bath ....   „

Cool or Cold Baths should as a rule be taken very quickly; Warm and Tepid Baths may be continued from 20 to 60 minutes, and are generally better during the latter part of the day; Cool or Cold Baths at Morning.

THE suitability of the different kinds of food in this table are indicated by a downward stroke, thus | , in front of the article or class intended ; where specially adapted two strokes are given, thus || ; where the article should be used with great caution or moderation a stroke underneath, thus —; and those which are not marked should be avoided.

ANIMAL FOOD.

Beef, roasted, broiled, &c.
Mutton, Lamb, &c., ditto.

Pork, Veal, Ham,
Water Fowls, or Ducks,
Geese, &c. &c., roast or broiled.

Chicken, Game, &c., roasted,
Bacon, well cured, fried or grilled,
Fish, cooked with fat, &c.
Shell-fish, as Oysters, Crabs, &c.

Eggs, lightly cooked with Bacon or fats.

Beef, boiled or stewed,
Mutton, ditto.

Pork, Ham, Water Fowls, &c. &c.,
boiled.

Chicken, Fowls, boiled.
Bacon, &c., boiled.

Eggs, boiled or poached.

FARINACEOUS SUBSTANCES.

Aërated Bread, stale,
Bread, only stale and pure,
Brown or Coarse Bread, stale,
Biscuits, Oat Bread, &c., ...
Fruit Pastry, well-made and eaten hot,
Light Farinaceous Puddings, i.e., Corn-
flour, Tapioca, Sago, Rice, Revalenta,
Ridge's Patent Food, light Suet Pud-
dings, &c.

Oatmeal and Coarse Flour in Porridges.

VEGETABLE FOOD.

Potatoes, dry and mealy
Beans, Peas, and Greens, Cabbages,
well-cooked.

Carrots, Turnips, Spinach,
Vegetable Marrows, Broccoli, &c. &c.

FRUITS.

Apples, Pears, Strawberries,
Currants, and other seed fruits, eaten
ripe and raw,
Ditto, ditto, cooked or in Pastry.

ANIMAL PRODUCTS.

Milk, for drinking,
Milk, as in Puddings, &c. &c.,
Butter or Cream, pure and good,
Cheese, Cream Cheese, &c.

SACCHARINE SUBSTANCES.

Sugar, pure,
Sweets, Preserved Fruits, &c.
Jams, &c. &c.

DRINKS.

Water, cold, pure, and soft,
Water, hot, with Milk and Sugar.
Tea, black only, and pure,
Coffee, pure,
Cocoa, Chocolate, &c.

Effervescing drinks, as Soda, Seltzer,
&c., are only suitable for certain
seasons and conditions.

Wines and Spirits, if taken, to be regarded medicinally, not as beverages.
Ales or Stout, if taken, to be regarded
only as an aid to Digestion and Assimilation, not as beverages.

Mr. HARRY LOBB'S special preparations: Mamalac, a food for Infants;
Phosphorized Cod Liver Oil, for Nervous and Glandular Debility ; Phosphorized
Food for weak Stomachs and Indigestion.

NOTE.—When the roasted or broiled meats in the above table are to be eaten, the food through should be chiefly solid; requiring good mastication. When boiled meats, stews, &c., are marked, soups and liquid substances may be taken more freely.

The number of meals taken per day must depend on the habits and constitution of the individual. As a rule those of consumptive or wasting types should take moderate meals frequently. The reverse with those of bilious and sanguineous habit. The number here marked gives an approximate idea of the number that may safely be taken.

Take .... meals per day.

The greater number of weak stomachs should avoid cold meats, cold puddings, cold pastry, &c. &c. This depends however on the chemical condition. If the alkalis predominate, the foods should be cool. If acids predominate, warm food is more suitable.

CLOTHING.

On this a good circulation chiefly depends, and many thousands, especially women, suffer ill-health from neglect on this point. A climate like that of England requires special attention to clothing; and the following is indicated as most suitable. A dash under the word indicates the mode.

Clothing should be part woollen,   all woollen,   thick woollen.

The parts requiring special protection are

CURATIVE AIDS:

MAGNETISM, ELECTRICITY, &c. &c.

Standing next to proper food and clothing comes the artificial aid of Electricity, chiefly in the form of Magnetism. The want of nervous power is the real source of all debility; and Magnetic Appliances, which, when worn as an ordinary garment, supply mild Electricity to the body, are unquestionably the best substitute and aid that modern science and medical skill have produced. Light and permanent magnets, scientifically polarized and encased in Woollen, Silk, or other materials, are worn over different parts, and by imparting magnetic warmth, set up and maintain a steady restorative action wherever debility exists. The following are a few of the ailments and derangements in which Magnetic Appliances have proved of the greatest value : Indigestion, Sluggish Liver, Spinal and General Debility, Bronchitis, Incipient or early Consumption, Paralysis or Loss of Power, Rheumatism, Lumbago, Neuralgia, Sciatica, Epilepsy, Loss of Circulation, Croup, Asthma, Pleurisy, Loss of Voice and Hearing, all forms of Glandular Swellings and Tumours, Dropsy, Wakefulness, Erysipelas, some forms of Headache, a Preventive or Palliative of Sea Sickness, and as a Preventive of Colds and Physical Depression.

As the wearing of these Appliances causes no more inconvenience than an ordinary garment, retain their curative power for years, and in most cases obviate all necessity for drugs and medicines, a "*Table of Health Directions*" would be incomplete without pointing out those most suitable.

Those marked in the following list with one dash, thus | , may be worn and used with advantage ; when with two dashes, thus ||, they are considered indispensable.

Spine Bands	Anklets
Belts, broad	Wristlets
Belts, ordinary	Magnetic Soles
Stomach and Liver Appliances	Friction Gloves
Lung Invigorators	Magnetic Caps
Chest Protectors	Corsets
Throat Protectors	Pads for general application
Sciatic Appliances	Leggins for cold legs
Arm Appliances	Appliances specially for weakness
Leg ditto	in the lower part of the body,
Knee Caps	female weakness, &c.

For *Price List see page 80 ; for Directions see other side.*

MAGNETISM,

AND

GENERAL DIRECTIONS FOR USING IT.

THE Appliances should be worn over the under garment, not next the body; they are equally effective worn in that manner, and are kept clean.

They may be worn at night as well as by day, if required, as their continued magnetic effect is often most beneficial.

They may be left off without danger of taking cold at any time, if some ordinary flannel or silk article of similar shape is worn as a substitute; in many cases they strengthen the parts so much, that in leaving them off no other article is necessary, and they can be put on again when advisable.

The only sensation generally imparted by wearing them is a glow of warmth; the warmth given indicates a restorative action, *is magnetic*, and therefore similar to the warmth produced by healthy blood, that has been oxygenated and magnetically warmed at the lungs.

As it may be thought by some that woollen and other garments "to promote warmth would be equally beneficial," it must be remembered that woollen, silk, &c. &c., only promote warmth by preventing the escape of heat. Many persons are deficient of natural heat, either general or local; clothing, however abundant, does not adequately warm them. THE MAGNETIC APPLIANCES INFUSE WARMTH FROM THE OUTSIDE, hence their superiority over every other form of inside garment where there is an insufficiency of heat.

To understand the value of Magnetic Appliances as curative agents, it must be remembered that *Heat is life*, in the sense that an absence of a proper degree of heat indicates a departure from health. In all cases where the standard balance of heat is absent from any portion of the body there is *a loss of Health to the part*; the obvious remedy is "to promote sufficient heat," this can always be done and maintained by magnetism.

The greater number of derangements and diseases in England arise from a humid atmosphere and damp soil, which abstract electricity and heat too rapidly from the body; woollen and silk garments are therefore highly necessary. And Magnetic Appliances, which maintain an equal circulation, by imparting electricity and heat from the outside, are unquestionably superior to all other curative agents.

For Price List see page 80.